Earth Science

THE STUDY OF SCIENCE

Earth Science

Edited by Maya Bayden

Britannica
Educational Publishing
IN ASSOCIATION WITH
ROSEN
EDUCATIONAL SERVICES

Published in 2017 by Britannica Educational Publishing (a trademark of Encyclopædia Britannica, Inc.) in association with The Rosen Publishing Group, Inc.
29 East 21st Street, New York, NY 10010

Distributed exclusively by Rosen Publishing.
To see additional Britannica Educational Publishing titles, go to rosenpublishing.com.

First Edition

Britannica Educational Publishing
J.E. Luebering: Executive Director, Core Editorial
Anthony L. Green: Editor, Compton's by Britannica

Rosen Publishing
Maya Bayden: Editor
Nelson Sá: Art Director
Brian Garvey: Designer
Cindy Reiman: Photography Manager
Bruce Donnola: Photo Researcher

Library of Congress Cataloging-in-Publication Data

Names: Bayden, Maya, editor.
Title: Earth science / edited by Maya Bayden.
Other titles: Study of science.
Description: First edition. | New York : Britannica Educational Publishing in association with Rosen Educational Services, 2017. | Series: The study of science | Includes bibliographical references and index.
Identifiers: LCCN 2016010601 | ISBN 9781680482263 (library bound : alk. paper)
Subjects: LCSH: Earth sciences—Juvenile literature. | Geology—Juvenile literature.
Classification: LCC QE29 .E259 2017 | DDC 550—dc23
LC record available at http://lccn.loc.gov/2016010601

Manufactured in China

Photo credits: Cover, p. 3 NASA/National Geographic Image Collection/Getty Images; p. 8 NASA/NOAA/GSFC/Suomi NPP/VIIRS/Norman Kuring; p. 14 Universal Images Group/Getty Images; p. 19 Eye Ubiquitous/Universal Images Group/Getty Images; pp. 21, 23, 25, 37, 50, 54-55, 62, 78, 104, 115, 126 Encyclopædia Britannica, Inc.; pp. 32, 44, 52 © Photos.com/Thinkstock; p. 34 Paul D. Stewart/Science Source; p. 42 © Hemera/Thinkstock; p. 56 Courtesy of The National Portrait Gallery, London; p. 59 Print Collector/Hulton Archive/Getty Images; p. 65 © World History Archive/Alamy Stock Photo; p. 72 NOAA Office of Coast Survey, U.S. Department of Commerce; p. 75 Time Life Pictures/The LIFE Pictures Collection/Getty Images; p. 80 NOAA; p. 85 The Lionel Pincus and Princess Firyal Map Division, New York Public Library; p. 91 Jonathan O'Neil; p. 95 Omikron/Science Source/Getty Images; p. 98 DEA/G. Cigolini/De Agostini/Getty Images; p. 101 Artwork: © Andrea Danti/Fotolia; p. 111 MCT/Tribune News Service/Getty Images; p. 119 Albert Moldvay/National Geographic Image Collection/Getty Images; p. 122 NOAA in Space Collection/National Oceanic and Atmospheric Administration (Image Number: spac0255); cover and interior pages backgrounds and borders © iStockphoto.com/LuMaxArt.

CONTENTS

INTRODUCTION 8

CHAPTER 1: ORIGINS OF THE EARTH SCIENCES 12
Geologic Sciences 12
Knowledge of Earth's Composition and Structure 13
Theophrastus 14
Zhang Heng 16
Knowledge of Earth History 17
Knowledge of Landforms and of Land-Sea Relations 18
Hydrologic and Atmospheric Sciences 21
Knowledge of the Water Cycle 22
The Origin of the Nile 24
Eratosthenes 26
Knowledge of the Tides 27
Prospecting for Groundwater 28

CHAPTER 2: THE 16TH–18TH CENTURIES 30
Geologic Sciences 30
Ore Deposits and Mineralogy 31
Georgius Agricola 32
Paleontology and Stratigraphy 33
Nicolaus Steno 36
The Neptunian and Plutonian Theories 38
Hydrologic Sciences 39
The Rise of Subterranean Water 39
Evaporation from the Sea 41
Atmospheric Sciences 42
Water Vapor in the Atmosphere 43
Otto von Guericke 44
Pressure, Temperature, and Atmospheric Circulation 45

Chapter 3: The 19th Century 48
Geologic Sciences 48
Crystallography and the Classification of Minerals and Rocks 49
William Smith and Faunal Succession 51
The Royal Society 53
Charles Lyell and Uniformitarianism 56
Charles Lyell 57
Louis Agassiz and the Ice Age 58
Louis Agassiz 60
Geologic Time and the Age of the Earth 61
Concepts of Landform Evolution 64
Gravity, Isostasy, and Earth's Figure 66
Hydrologic Sciences 67
Darcy's Law 68
Henri Darcy 69
Surface Water Discharge 70
Foundations of Oceanography 71
Atmospheric Sciences 75
Composition of the Atmosphere 76
Understanding of Clouds, Fog, and Dew 77
Observation and Study of Storms 79
Weather and Climate 82
Weather Maps 84

Chapter 4: The 20th Century to the Present: Modern Trends and Developments 87
Geologic Sciences 88
Radiometric Dating 88
Bertram Boltwood 89

Experimental Study of Rocks 92
Crystallography 94
Chemical Analysis of Rocks and Minerals 96
Micropaleontology 97
Seismology and the Structure of Earth 99
Andrija Mohorovičić 100
The Theory of Plate Tectonics 102
Hydrologic Sciences 108
Water Resources and Seawater Chemistry 108
Desalinization, Tidal Power, and Minerals from the Sea 110
Ocean Bathymetry 112
Ocean Circulation, Currents, and Waves 113
Glacier Motion and High-Latitude Ice Sheets 117
Atmospheric Sciences 119
Probes, Satellites, and Data Transmission 120
Weather Forecasting 122
John von Neumann *123*
Cloud Physics 124
Properties and Structure of the Atmosphere 125
Weather Modification 127

Conclusion **129**

Glossary **131**

For More Information **134**

For Further Reading **138**

Index **140**

INTRODUCTION

The earth sciences seek to understand the physical features of Earth and how they developed, and in turn, to use that knowledge to benefit humans.

The earth sciences comprise the fields of study concerned with the solid Earth, its waters, and the air that envelops it. These fields include the geologic sciences, hydrologic sciences, and atmospheric sciences, respectively.

The broad aim of the earth sciences is to understand Earth's present features and its past evolution, and to use this knowledge, when possible, to benefit humankind. Thus, earth scientists observe, describe, and classify all the features of Earth to generate hypotheses with which to explain how and why Earth's features developed as they did and to check opposing ideas for their relative validity. In this way, the most plausible, acceptable, and long-lasting ideas are developed.

The physical environment in which humans live includes not only the immediate surface of Earth but also the ground beneath it and the water and air above it. Early humans were more involved with the practicalities of life than with theories. Their survival depended on the ability to obtain metals from the ground to produce alloys, such as bronze from copper and tin, for tools; to find adequate water supplies to establish dwelling sites; and to forecast the weather, which had a far greater bearing on human life in earlier times than it has today. Such situations were the foundations of the three main components of the modern earth sciences.

The rapid development of science as a whole over the past century and a half has given rise to an immense number of specializations and subdisciplines. As a result, modern earth scientists usually know a great deal about a very small area of study but only a little about other aspects of the entire field. Accordingly, it is important for the layperson and researcher alike to be aware of the complex interlinking network of disciplines that make up the earth sciences today. Only when one is aware of the marvelous complexity of the earth sciences and yet can understand the breakdown of the component disciplines is one able to choose those parts of the subject that are of greatest interest.

It is worth emphasizing two important features common to all three divisions of the earth sciences. First is that many objects of study are inaccessible. Many rocks, as well as water and oil reservoirs, are at great depths below Earth's surface; air masses circulate at vast heights above it. Therefore, the earth scientist must have a good three-dimensional perspective. Second, all fields of the earth sciences are subject to time. The earth scientist is responsible for understanding how Earth evolved over millions of years. For example, what were the physical and chemical conditions on Earth 3.5 billion years ago? How did the oceans form, and how did their chemical composition change with time? How has the atmosphere developed? And finally, how did life on Earth begin, and from what did humans evolve?

There are many subdivisions of the earth sciences beyond the three main disciplines, and different approaches divide subfields of study in a variety of ways. With such a merging across subdisciplines, researchers today must be adaptable in their approach to problems. A key aspect of training within the earth sciences is an appreciation of their multidisciplinary nature.

ORIGINS OF THE EARTH SCIENCES

The origins of the earth sciences lie in the myths and legends of the distant past. The creation story, or the story of how Earth came to exist, can be traced to a Babylonian epic of the twenty-second century BCE. Retold in the first chapter of the biblical book of Genesis, the story has proved most influential. The story is cast in the form of Earth history and so was widely accepted by ancient cultures as both scientific and religious truth.

Earth scientists later made countless observations about natural phenomena. Such observations were examined through various fields of study. However, the earth sciences were slow to develop. This was largely because scientific advances were restricted by whatever society tolerated or supported.

GEOLOGIC SCIENCES

Geology is concerned with the solid Earth—its history, its shape, the materials forming it, and the processes that are acting and have acted on it. Geologists are concerned primarily with rocks and materials derived from rocks that make up the outer part of Earth. To understand these materials, geologists incorporate knowledge from other fields of science, such as physics, chemistry, and biology; thus, geological fields—such as geophysics, geochemistry, geochronology, and paleontology—incorporate other sciences, enabling geologists to understand better the working of Earth processes through time. The human study of rocks dates to the first millennium BCE.

Knowledge of Earth's Composition and Structure

The oldest known treatise on rocks and minerals is *De lapidibus* (On stones). It was written by the Greek philosopher Theophrastus (ca. 372–ca. 287 BCE) probably in the early years of the third century BCE. For almost two thousand years it remained the best study of minerals. Although the work refers only to about seventy different materials, its main achievement was in attempting a classification system of rocks and minerals.

In early Chinese writings on mineralogy, stones and rocks were distinguished from

THEOPHRASTUS

Theophrastus (ca. 372–ca. 287 BCE) was a Greek Peripatetic philosopher and student of Aristotle's. He studied at Athens under Aristotle; when Aristotle was forced to retire in 323, Theophrastus became the head of the Lyceum, the academy in Athens founded by Aristotle. Under Theophrastus, the number of pupils and auditors studying at the Lyceum rose to its highest point.

Theophrastus

Because Aristotle walked about while teaching, his school was called the Peripatetic (which means "to walk about") school. Aristotle led his pupils, including Theophrastus, in research in every existing field of knowledge. They dissected animals and studied the habits of insects. The science of observation was new to the Greeks. Hampered by lack of instruments, they were not always correct in their conclusions.

Theophrastus was one of the few Peripatetics who fully embraced Aristotle's philosophy in all areas of metaphysics, physics, physiology, zoology, botany, ethics, politics, and history of culture. His general tendency was to strengthen the systematic unity of those subjects. His works included *Peri phyton historia* (Inquiry into plants), *Peri phyton aition* (Growth of plants), and *De lapidibus* (On stones), the first treatise on rocks and minerals.

metals and alloys. Further distinctions were made on the basis of color and other physical properties. The beliefs of Zheng Sixiao (died 1332 CE) on the origin of ore deposits were more advanced than those of Europeans of his time. In brief, he suggested that ore was deposited from groundwater flowing in cracks beneath Earth's surface.

Ancient accounts of earthquakes and volcanic eruptions are sometimes valuable as historical records but tell little about the causes of these events. Aristotle (384–322 BCE) and Strabo (64 BCE–ca. 21 CE) held that volcanic explosions and earthquakes were caused by irregular motions of hot winds that move underground and occasionally burst forth in volcanic activity. Classical and medieval ideas on earthquakes and volcanoes were brought together in William Caxton's *Mirrour of the World* (1480). Here again, earthquakes are related to movements of fluids under the planet's surface. Streams of water in the earth compress air in hidden caverns. If the roofs of the caverns are weak, they collapse, causing cities and castles to fall into the chasms; if strong, they merely tremble and shake from the movement of the wind below. According to Caxton, volcanic action follows if the outburst of wind and water from the depths is accompanied by fire and brimstone from hell.

Zhang Heng

Zhang Heng (78–139 CE) was a Chinese mathematician, astronomer, and geographer. As early as 132 CE, he invented the seismoscope, an early seismic instrument. The instrument could not record the time of ground vibrations, but it did indicate that shaking had occurred. Zhang's seismoscope was cylindrical in shape, with eight dragon heads arranged around its upper circumference, each with a ball in its mouth. Below were eight frogs, each directly under a dragon head. When an earthquake occurred, a ball dropped and was caught by a frog's mouth, generating a sound.

More so than any other ancient civilization, the Chinese kept faithful records of earthquakes. Records of the dates on which major quakes rocked China date back to 780 BCE. The Chinese also invented the first instrument capable of detecting earthquakes at a distance: the first seismograph, invented by the mathematician, astronomer, and geographer Zhang Heng (78–139 CE).

Knowledge of Earth History

Seashells found embedded in the hard rocks of high mountains aroused the curiosity of early naturalists and eventually set off a controversy on the origin of fossils that continued through the seventeenth century. Xenophanes of Colophon (flourished ca. 560 BCE) was credited by later writers with observing that seashells occur "in the midst of earth and in mountains." He is said to have believed that these relics were the result of a catastrophic event that caused earth to be mixed with the sea and then to settle, burying organisms in the drying mud. For these views, Xenophanes is sometimes called the father of paleontology.

Petrified wood was described by Chinese scholars as early as the ninth century CE.

About 1080, the scientist Shen Kuo claimed fossilized plants were evidence of change in climate. Other kinds of fossils that attracted the attention of early Chinese writers include spiriferoid brachiopods ("stone swallows"), cephalopods, crabs, and the bones and teeth of reptiles, birds, and mammals. Although these objects were commonly collected simply as curiosities or for medicinal purposes, Shen Kuo recognized marine invertebrate fossils for what they are and for what they imply historically. Observing seashells in strata of the Taihang Mountains, he concluded that this region, though now far from the sea, must once have encompassed a shoreline.

KNOWLEDGE OF LANDFORMS AND OF LAND-SEA RELATIONS

Some early writers were aware of changes in the landscape and in the position of land and sea related to erosion and sediment repeatedly deposited and eroded by streams. The Greek historian Herodotus (ca. 484–ca. 426 BCE) correctly concluded that the northward bulge of Egypt into the Mediterranean is caused by mud carried and deposited by the Nile.

Early Chinese writers also understood the changes caused by erosion. In the *Jinshu*

A statue of Greek historian Herodotus sits in front of the Parliament Building in Vienna, Austria.

(History of the Jin dynasty), it is said that military general Du Yu (222–284 CE) had monumental stone slabs carved with the records of his successes and that he had one buried at the foot of a mountain and the other erected on top. He predicted that in time they would likely change their relative positions, because the high hills would become valleys and the deep valleys would become hills.

Aristotle guessed that changes in the position of land and sea might occur in a cycle, which implies some sort of natural order. If the rivers of a wet region built deltas at their mouths, he reasoned, the level of the sea would rise and water would cover some adjacent dry region. A reversal of climatic conditions might then cause a lowering of sea level, and water would retreat from the area previously flooded.

The idea of a cyclical interchange between land and sea was developed in the *Epistles of the Brethren of Purity and Loyal Friends*, a classic Arabic work written sometime in the second half of the tenth century CE by an anonymous group of scholars at Basra, Iraq. The rocks of the lands disintegrate, and rivers carry this sediment to the sea. Waves and currents then spread it over the seafloor. There the layers of sediment accumulate one on top of the other. The layers harden, and, in the course of time, rise from the bottom of the sea to form new continents. Then the process of disintegration and leveling starts over.

Hydrologic and Atmospheric Sciences

The only substance known to the ancient philosophers in its solid, liquid, and gaseous states was water. It is, therefore, prominently featured in early theories about the origin of Earth and how Earth operates. Thales of Miletus (ca. 624–ca. 545 BCE) is credited with a belief that water is the essential substance of

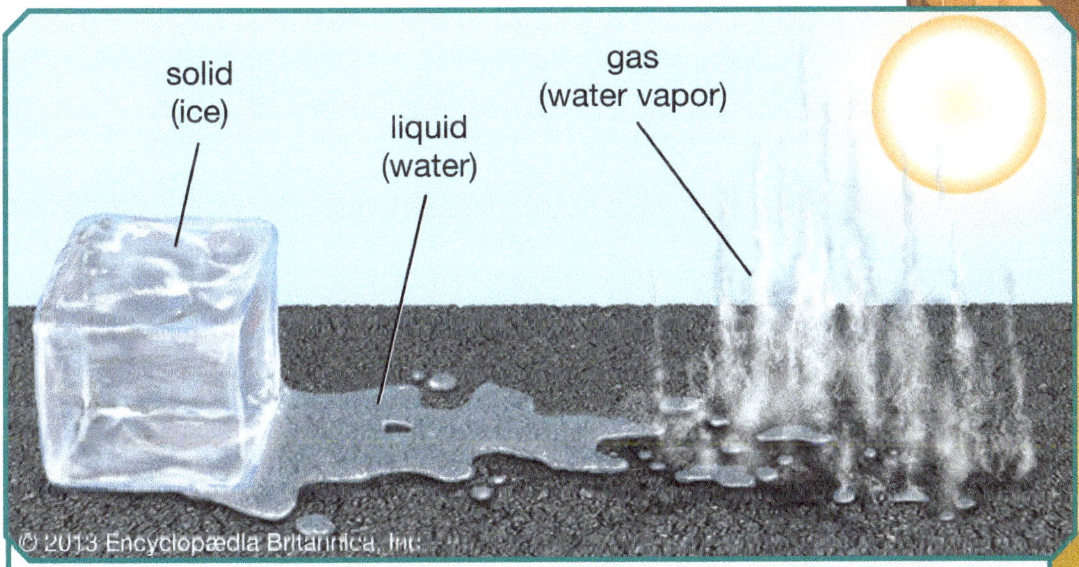

Water was the only substance known to the ancient philosophers in its three states—as ice (solid), liquid water, and water vapor (gas). (Like all gases, water vapor is invisible; it is shown here merely for the purpose of illustration.)

Earth. Anaximander of Miletus (ca. 610–545 BCE) held that water was probably the source of life. In the system proposed by Empedocles of Agrigentum (c. 490–430 BCE), water shared the primacy Thales had given it with three other elements: fire, air, and earth. The doctrine of the four earthly elements later became part of the universal system of Aristotle, thereby influencing Western scientific thought until the late seventeenth century.

KNOWLEDGE OF THE WATER CYCLE

The idea that the waters of Earth undergo a cycle—changing from seawater to vapor to precipitation (such as rain and snow) and then flowing back to the ocean—is probably older than any of the surviving texts that hint at or frame it explicitly. This process is known as the hydrological or water cycle.

The idea of the water cycle developed independently in China as early as the fourth century BCE. It was explicitly stated in the *Lüshi chunqiu* (The spring and autumn annals of Mr. Lü), written in the third century BCE. Plato (ca. 428–348/347 BCE) theorized a circulatory system of a different kind, one that involved movements of water on a large scale within Earth. In one of his two explanations for the origin of rivers and springs, he described Earth as perforated by passages connecting with Tartarus, a vast underground water reservoir.

A sound theory of precipitation is found in the writings of Aristotle. Moisture on Earth is changed to airy vapor by heat from above. Because heat rises, the heat in the

Earth's water is constantly recycled. It falls on the land as rain and snow, is carried by rivers or groundwater to the oceans, rises as water vapor, and travels inland again. This process is called the water cycle.

vapor carries it upward. When the heat begins to leave the vapor, the vapor turns to water. The formation of water from air produces clouds. Heat remaining in the clouds is further opposed by the cold inherent in the water and is driven away. The cold presses the particles of the cloud closer together, restoring in them the true nature of the element water. Water naturally moves downward, and so it falls from the cloud as raindrops. Snow falls from clouds that have frozen.

In Aristotle's system, the four earthly elements were not stable; they could change into one another. Thus if air can change to water in the sky, it should also be able to change into water underground.

THE ORIGIN OF THE NILE

Of all the rivers known in the ancient world, the Nile was most puzzling with regard to its sources of water. The river's course runs the length of Egypt through a virtually rainless desert, but it rises regularly in flood once each year.

There were many varied theories on the strange behavior of the Nile, though they were mostly wrong. Thales suggested that the strong winds that blow southward over the delta in the summer hold back the flow of the river, causing the waters to rise and flood. Oenopides of Chios (flourished ca. 475 BCE) thought that heat stored in the ground during the winter dries up the underground veins of water so that the river shrinks. In the summer, the heat disappears, and water flows up into the river, causing floods. In the view of Diogenes of Apollonia (flourished ca. 435 BCE), the sun controls the regimen of the stream.

The world's longest river, the Nile rises south of the equator and flows northward through northeastern Africa to drain into the Mediterranean Sea.

The idea that the Nile waters connect with the sea is an old one. It can be traced back to the geographic concepts of Hecataeus of Miletus (ca. 520 BCE). Reasonable explanations insisted there was a relationship between the discharge of the Nile and precipitation near its source, as snow (Anaxagoras of Clazomenae, ca. 500–428 BCE) or from rain that filled lakes

ERATOSTHENES

The Greek scientist Eratosthenes was the first person to calculate Earth's circumference. He worked as chief librarian of the Alexandrian Library in Egypt and was also known as a writer, an astronomer, a mathematician, and a poet.

Born about 276 BCE in Cyrene, in what is now Libya, Eratosthenes studied in Alexandria and Athens, Greece. He settled in Alexandria about 255 BCE and became director of the city's great library. He worked out a calendar that included leap years, and he tried to fix the dates of literary and political events since the siege of Troy. His writings include a poem inspired by astronomy as well as works on the theater and on ethics. Eratosthenes was also credited with some groundbreaking work in geography, including a relatively accurate sketch of the Nile River.

Eratosthenes noticed that the sunlight in Alexandria fell at an angle of about 7 percent from the vertical at noon on the summer solstice, while 500 miles (800 kilometers) to the southeast, in what is now Aswan, Egypt, the sun's rays fell vertically. He correctly assumed the sun's distance to be very great; its rays therefore are practically parallel when they reach Earth. Given estimates of the distance between the two cities, he was able to calculate the circumference of Earth. The exact length of the units (stadia) he used is doubtful, and the accuracy of his result is therefore uncertain; it may have varied by 0.5 to 17 percent from the value accepted by modern astronomers. He also measured the tilt of Earth's axis with great accuracy and compiled a star catalog. His mathematical work is known principally from the writings of Pappus of Alexandria.

Eratosthenes also created a prime number procedure known as the sieve of Eratosthenes. This tool is still used in number theory research. In his old age, Eratosthenes suffered from blindness, and he is said to have committed suicide by voluntary starvation. He died in Alexandria about 194 BCE.

thought to then feed the river (Democritus of Abdera, ca. 460–ca. 357 BCE). Eratosthenes (ca. 276–194 BCE), who had prepared a map of the Nile valley southward to the latitude of modern Khartoum, anticipated the correct answer when he reported that heavy rains had been observed to fall in the upper reaches of the river and that these were sufficient to account for the flooding.

Knowledge of the Tides

The tides of the Mediterranean, inconspicuous in most places, attracted little notice from Greek and Roman naturalists, though it was a Greek naturalist—Poseidonius (135–50 BCE)—who first related changes in the tides to the phases of the moon. By contrast, the tides along the eastern shores of Asia generally have a considerable range and were closely observed by the Chinese. In particular, the tidal bore on the Qiantang River near Hangzhou attracted early attention. With its front ranging up to 12 feet (3.7 meters) in height, this bore is one of the largest in the world. As early as the second century BCE, the Chinese had recognized a connection between tides and tidal bores and the lunar cycle.

PROSPECTING FOR GROUNDWATER

The arts of finding and managing groundwater were highly developed in the eighth century BCE. The construction of long, hand-dug underground aqueducts (known as *qanat*s) in Armenia and Persia represents one of the great hydrologic achievements of the ancient world. After some three thousand years, *qanat*s are still a major source of water in Iran.

In the first century BCE, Vitruvius (Marcus Vitruvius Pollio), a Roman architect and engineer, described methods of exploring for groundwater in his *De architectura libri decem* (*The Architecture of Marcus Vitruvius*

Pollio, in Ten Books). To locate places where wells should be dug, he recommended looking for spots where mist rises in early morning. More significantly, Vitruvius had learned to associate different quantities and qualities of groundwater with different kinds of rocks and topographic situations.

After the inspired beginnings of the ancient Greeks, Romans, Chinese, and Arabs, scientific discovery slowed during the Middle Ages. It was not until the Renaissance in the early sixteenth century that scientific thought once again began to flourish.

THE 16TH–18TH CENTURIES

The Renaissance brought new energy to all avenues of intellectual thought, and in no area was this more apparent than in the sciences. Novel approaches to science and the waning influence of religious doctrine over scientific ideas gave way to important new theories in geology, hydrology, and atmospheric sciences.

GEOLOGIC SCIENCES

The Renaissance and early Modern period brought new understanding of how strata (rock layers) form and how ancient organic materials became fossilized. Different theories developed on how the movement of strata relates to changes in the position of fossils, leading to differing theories on the origins of Earth.

ORE DEPOSITS AND MINERALOGY

In the sixteenth and seventeenth centuries, alchemists held the popular belief that metal deposits were made by heat coming from the center of Earth but activated by the heavenly bodies.

In several of his works, the sixteenth-century German scientist Georgius Agricola describes his ideas on the origin of ore deposits in veins and correctly attributes them to deposition from aqueous solution. He also describes in detail the erosive action of rivers and its effect in the shaping of mountains. Of his seven books on geology, *De natura fossilium* (1546; On natural fossils) contains his major contributions to mineralogy. In Agricola's time and well into the nineteenth century, "fossil" was a term that could be applied to any object dug from the earth. Thus, Agricola's classification of fossils included organic remains, such as ammonites, and rocks of various kinds in addition to minerals.

With the birth of analytical chemistry in the late eighteenth century, it became possible to analyze minerals based on their composition. The German geologist

Georgius Agricola

Georgius Agricola (1494–1555) was a German scholar and scientist known as the father of mineralogy. A highly educated classicist and humanist, well regarded by scholars of his own and later times, he was yet singularly independent of the theories of ancient authorities. He was indeed among the first to found a natural science upon observation, as opposed to speculation. His *De re metallica* (*On the Nature of Metals*) dealt chiefly with the arts of mining and smelting. His *De natura fossilium* (*On Natural Fossils*), considered the first mineralogy textbook, presented the first scientific classification of minerals (based on their physical properties) and described many new minerals, their occurrence and mutual relationships.

Georgius Agricola

In *De re metallica* (published posthumously in 1556), Agricola was mainly concerned with mining and metallurgy. He discussed the geology of ore bodies, surveying, mine construction, pumping, and ventilation. There is much on the application of waterpower. He describes the assaying of ores, the methods used for enriching ores

before smelting, and procedures for smelting and refining a number of metals. He concludes with a discussion of the production of glass and of a variety of chemicals used in smelting operations.

In *De natura fossilium,* Agricola offers a classification of minerals (called "fossils" at that time) in terms of geometric form (spheres, cones, plates). He was probably the first to distinguish between "simple" substances and "compounds." In Agricola's day, chemical knowledge was almost nonexistent, and there was no proper chemical analysis (other than analysis of ores by the use of fire), so the classification of ores was necessarily crude.

Abraham Gottlob Werner was one of those who favored a chemical classification over a "natural history" classification based on external appearances. His list of several classifications, published after his death, recognized 317 different substances ordered in four classes.

Paleontology and Stratigraphy

During the seventeenth century, the guiding principles of paleontology and historical geology began to emerge in the work of a few individuals. The Danish scientist Nicolaus Steno presented carefully reasoned arguments

When Nicolaus Steno discovered large triangular objects (as illustrated above) in rock layers in Malta, he concluded that they were the fossilized teeth of sharks.

in favor of the organic, or living, origin of what are now called fossils.

Steno also clarified three principles that made it possible to reconstruct certain kinds of geologic events in a chronological order. In his *Canis carcariae dissectum caput* (1667; Dissected head of a dog shark), he concluded that large tongue-shaped objects found in the strata of Malta were the teeth of sharks, whose remains had been buried beneath the seafloor and later raised out of the water to their present sites. This conclusion led Steno to confront a broader question. How can one solid body, such as a shark's tooth, become embedded in another solid body, such as a layer of rock?

In 1669, Steno published his answers to that question in a paper titled "De solido intra naturaliter contento dissertationis" (A preliminary discourse concerning a solid body enclosed by processes of nature within a solid). Steno explained that when the hard parts of an organism are covered with sediment, it is the organism's parts that are firm, not the layers of sediment. The sediment may harden into rock later, and, if so, the original solid fossil becomes contained within solid rock. He recognized that sediments settle

NICOLAUS STENO

Nicolaus Steno (1638–1686) was a Danish geologist and anatomist whose early observations greatly advanced the development of geology. After studying human anatomy in Amsterdam in the early 1660s, Steno went in 1665 to Florence, where he was the physician of Grand Duke Ferdinand II. Steno traveled extensively in Italy, and in 1669, he published his geological observations in *De solido intra naturaliter contento dissertationis* (*A Preliminary Discourse Concerning a Solid Body Enclosed by Processes of Nature Within a Solid*). In this fundamental work of geology, Steno laid the foundations of the science of crystallography. He reported that, although quartz crystals differ greatly in physical appearance, they all have the same angles between corresponding faces.

Steno was the first to realize that Earth's crust contains a chronological history of geologic events and that the history may be deciphered by careful study of its layers (called strata) and fossils. He rejected the idea that mountains grow like trees, proposing instead that they are formed by changes to Earth's crust. Furthermore, he put forward the revolutionary idea that fossils are the remains of ancient living organisms. Though Steno was not the only naturalist of his day to propose this idea, he was the first to argue that fossils were snapshots of life at different times in Earth's history, and that rock layers formed slowly over time.

from fluids layer by layer, forming strata that are originally continuous and nearly horizontal. He further states that in a sequence of strata, as originally laid down, any stratum is younger than the one on which it rests and older than the one that rests upon it. This idea forms the basis of the law of superposition, one of the most important principles in geology.

In 1667 and 1668 the English physicist Robert Hooke read papers before the Royal Society (a leading British scientific society) in which he expressed many of the ideas in Steno's works. Hooke argued that fossils were once organic. He explained how beds containing

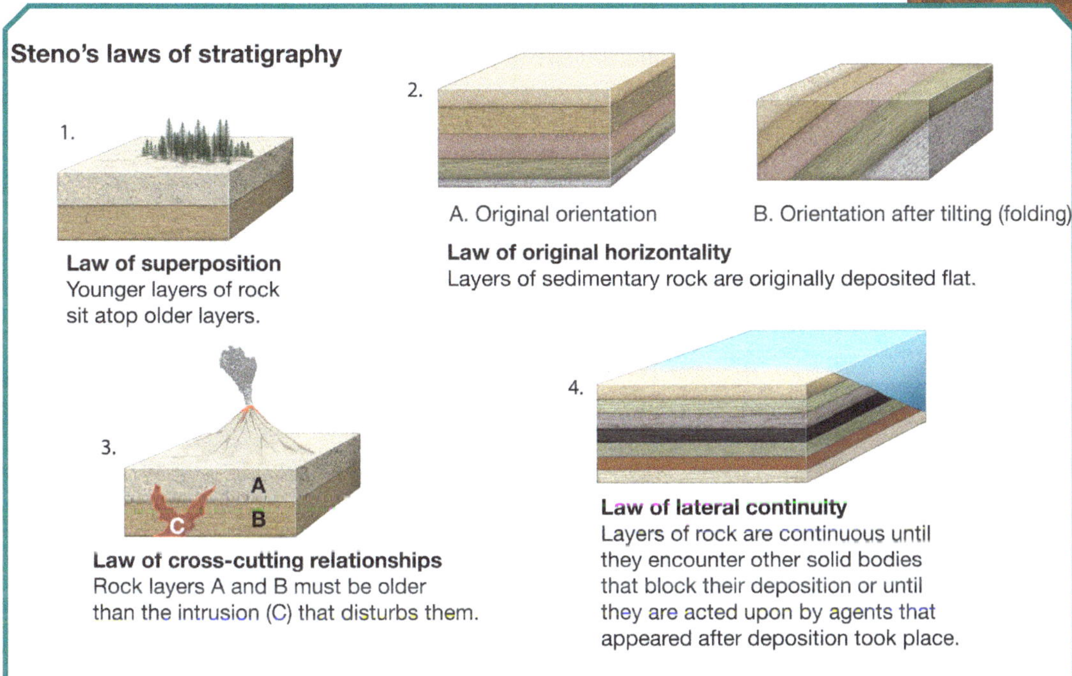

Steno's four laws of stratigraphy made it possible to work out the superpositional relationships within rock sequences as well as the relative age of each layer.

marine fossils could reach mountainous heights as a result of earthquakes. Streams then wear down the hills, fill lower areas with sediment, and thus level out irregularities in the landscape.

THE NEPTUNIAN AND PLUTONIAN THEORIES

The two major theories of Earth history in the eighteenth century were the Neptunian and the Plutonian. The Neptunists, led by Abraham Gottlob Werner and his students, believed that Earth was originally covered by a dirt- and mud-filled ocean. The first sediments deposited on the floor of this universal ocean formed granite and other crystalline rocks. Then as the ocean began to subside, stratified (layered) rocks were laid down one after another.

The Scottish scientist James Hutton, leader of the Plutonists, viewed Earth as a dynamic body that functions as a heat machine. Streams wear down the continents and deposit their waste in the sea. Heat below Earth's surface causes the outer part of Earth to expand in places, elevating the compacted marine sediments to form new continents. Hutton found evidence for many of his claims, including the driving force of subterranean heat (that is, heat below Earth's surface). His *Theory of the Earth* was first published as an essay in 1788. In 1795, it was expanded to a two-volume work. John Playfair, a professor of natural philosophy, defended Hutton against the Neptunists; his *Illustrations of the Huttonian Theory* (1802) is the clearest contemporary account of Plutonist theory.

Hydrologic Sciences

The idea that there is a circulatory system within Earth, by which seawater is brought to mountaintops and released there, continued until early in the eighteenth century. Two questions that this theory did not resolve were widely acknowledged. How is seawater forced uphill? How is the salt lost in the process?

The Rise of Subterranean Water

The French mathematician and scientist René Descartes supposed that seawater ran through subterranean channels into large caverns below the tops of mountains. Jesuit philosopher Athanasius Kircher suggested in his *Mundus subterraneus* (1664; Subterranean world) that the ocean tides pump seawater through hidden channels to points of outlet at springs. To explain the rise of subterranean water beneath mountains, the chemist Robert Plot appealed to the pressure of air, which forces water up the insides of mountains. The idea of a great subterranean sea connecting with the ocean and supplying it with water together with all springs and rivers was resurrected in 1695 in John Woodward's *Essay Towards a Natural History of the Earth and Terrestrial Bodies*.

In contrast, French scientist Bernard Palissy maintained that rainfall is the only source of rivers and springs. In his *Discours admirables* (1580; *Admirable Discourses*) he described how rainwater falling on mountains enters cracks in the ground. It then flows down along these cracks until an obstruction blocks its path. At that point, it flows out on the surface as springs. Palissy rejected the idea that seawater rises in veins to the tops of mountains. For this to be true, sea level would have to be higher than mountaintops—an impossibility. In his *Discours,* Palissy suggested that water would rise above the level at which it was first found in a well if the source of the groundwater came from a place higher than the bottom of the well. This is an early reference to conditions under which an artesian well works, a popular subject among Italian hydrologists of the seventeenth and eighteenth centuries.

In the late seventeenth century, Pierre Perrault and Edmé Mariotte conducted hydrologic investigations in the basin of the Seine River that established that the local annual precipitation was more than ample to account for the annual runoff.

EVAPORATION FROM THE SEA

The question remained as to whether enough water is evaporated from the sea to account for the precipitation that feeds the streams. The English astronomer and mathematician Edmond Halley measured the rate of evaporation from pans of water exposed to the air during hot summer days. Assuming that this same rate would be true for the Mediterranean Sea, Halley calculated that some 5.28 billion tons of water are evaporated from that body during a summer day. Assuming further that each of the nine major rivers flowing into the Mediterranean has a daily discharge ten times that of the Thames, he calculated that a daily inflow of fresh water back into that sea would

Edmond Halley

be 1.827 billion tons, only slightly more than a third of the amount lost by evaporation. Halley proposed that part of the remaining water returns to the sea as rain before it reaches land. Another part is taken up by plants.

In the course of the hydrologic cycle, Halley reasoned, the rivers constantly bring salt into the sea in solution, but the salt is left behind when seawater evaporates to replenish the streams with rainwater. Thus in this scenario, the sea must be growing steadily saltier.

ATMOSPHERIC SCIENCES

Advances in the atmospheric sciences came in the eighteenth century as the understanding arose that (1) water vapor and air are not, in fact, the same substance, and (2) air has weight.

This knowledge led to the development of theories on air pressure and air circulation.

Water Vapor in the Atmosphere

After 1760 the analytical chemists finally demonstrated that water and air are not the same substance. Long before this development, however, investigators had begun to draw a distinction between water vapor and air. The German physicist Otto von Guericke produced artificial clouds by releasing air from one flask into another one from which the air had been evacuated. A fog then formed in the unevacuated flask. Guericke concluded that air couldn't be turned into water, though moisture can enter the air and later be condensed into water.

Guericke's experiments, however, did not answer the question as to how water enters the atmosphere as vapor. In "Les Météores" ("Meteorology," an essay published in the book *Discours de la methode* in 1637), Descartes pictured water as made up of small particles that were elongated, smooth, and separated by a highly rarified "subtle matter."

The same uncertainty as to how water gets into the air surrounded the question as to how it remains suspended as clouds. A popular view in the eighteenth century was that clouds are

OTTO VON GUERICKE

The German physicist, engineer, and natural philosopher Otto von Guericke (1602–1686) was responsible for developing many revolutionary ideas in modern science. He was the first to recognize the concept of the vacuum in physics. He invented the first air pump and used it to study the phenomenon of vacuum and the role of air in combustion and respiration.

Born in Magdeburg, Prussian Saxony (now in Germany), on Nov. 20, 1602, Guericke was educated at the University of Leipzig; he studied law at the University of Jena and mathematics and mechanics at the University of Leyden. In 1631, he became an engineer in the army of Gustavus II Adolphus of Sweden. From 1646 to 1681, he was mayor of Magdeburg and magistrate for Brandenburg.

In 1650, Guericke performed his first air pump and vacuum experiments. His studies revealed that light travels through a vacuum but sound does not. In a famous series

Title page of *Experimenta Nova (ut vocantur) Magdeburgica de Vacuo Spatio* ("New Magdeburg experiments about the vacuum"), 1672, in which Otto von Guericke published details of his invention of the air pump and the power of air pressure.

of experiments in 1654, Guericke placed two copper bowls together to form a hollow sphere about 14 inches (36 centimeters) in diameter. After he had removed the air from the sphere, horses were unable to pull the bowls apart, even though the bowls were held together only by the air around them. This was the first demonstration of the tremendous force that air pressure exerts.

Guericke had major achievements in other areas of science as well. In 1663, he invented the first electric generator, which produced static electricity by applying friction against a revolving ball of sulfur. He discovered in 1672 that the electricity produced this way could cause the surface of the sulfur ball to glow, a phenomenon known as electroluminescence. He also studied astronomy and predicted that comets would return regularly from outer space. Guericke died on May 11, 1686, in Hamburg.

made of countless tiny bubbles that float in air. Guericke had suggested that the fine particles in his artificial clouds were bubbles. Other observers claimed to have seen bubble-shaped particles of water vapor rising from warm water or hot coffee.

Pressure, Temperature, and Atmospheric Circulation

If clouds are essentially balloons with many compartments, their motions could be explained by the movements of winds blowing on them. Descartes suggested that the winds might blow upward as well as to the side. This would explain how clouds rise or at least why they do not fall. In 1749, Benjamin Franklin explained updrafts of air as due to local heating of the atmosphere by the sun.

Sixteen years later, the Swiss-German physicist Johann Heinrich Lambert described the conditions necessary for convection currents to begin in the atmosphere. He reasoned that rising warm air flows into areas of cooler air. This causes an increase in the cooler air's downward pressure, and causes its lower layers to flow into rising currents. The result is air circulation.

The fact that Lambert could explain circulation as an effect of changes in air pressure reflects an important change from the outdated view that air was weightless. This misconception was corrected after 1643 with the invention of the mercury barometer—an instrument for measuring air pressure. It was soon discovered that the height of the barometer varied with the weather: it stood at its highest during clear weather and fell to its lowest on rainy days.

Toward the end of the eighteenth century, it was beginning to be understood that variations in the barometer must be related to the general motion and circulation of the atmosphere. The Swiss scientist Horace Bénédict de Saussure concluded in his *Essais sur l'hygrométrie* (1783; Essay on hygrometry) that these variations could not be due solely to changes in humidity. From experiments with changes of water vapor and pressure in air contained in a glass globe, Saussure concluded that changes in temperature must be immediately responsible for variations of the barometer and that these in turn must be related to the movement of air from one place to another.

THE 19TH CENTURY

The nineteenth century was a period of expansion of knowledge both upward and downward as scientists furthered their investigation of Earth, its atmosphere, and its waters. Advances in geology brought improved understanding of Earth's composition and what its study could successfully reveal to us about the planet's history and organisms. Likewise, new explorations of the oceans, streams, and groundwater fueled new revelations about marine life and the freshwater sources upon which human populations relied. In the atmospheric sciences, the focus largely turned to weather patterns—both understanding and predicting them.

GEOLOGIC SCIENCES

In the nineteenth century, advances in geology centered on improved classification of mineral and rock strata. This led to the development of the law of faunal succession, which states that groups of fossils follow each other in time in a predictable manner. This proved to be an important step in establishing geology's ability to compare strata at great geographic distance. This principle coupled with other scientific developments led to a much-improved understanding of geologic time and also of how landscapes form.

Crystallography and the Classification of Minerals and Rocks

The French scientist René-Just Häuy wrote papers on mineralogy and crystallography in 1801 and 1822, respectively. As a result, he is credited with advancing mineralogy to the status of a science and with establishing the science of crystallography—the study of crystals. From his geometric studies of minerals, he concluded that the particles forming a given species of mineral have the same shape. Furthermore, he concluded that differences in the external shape of crystals reflect differences in the ways identical molecules are put together.

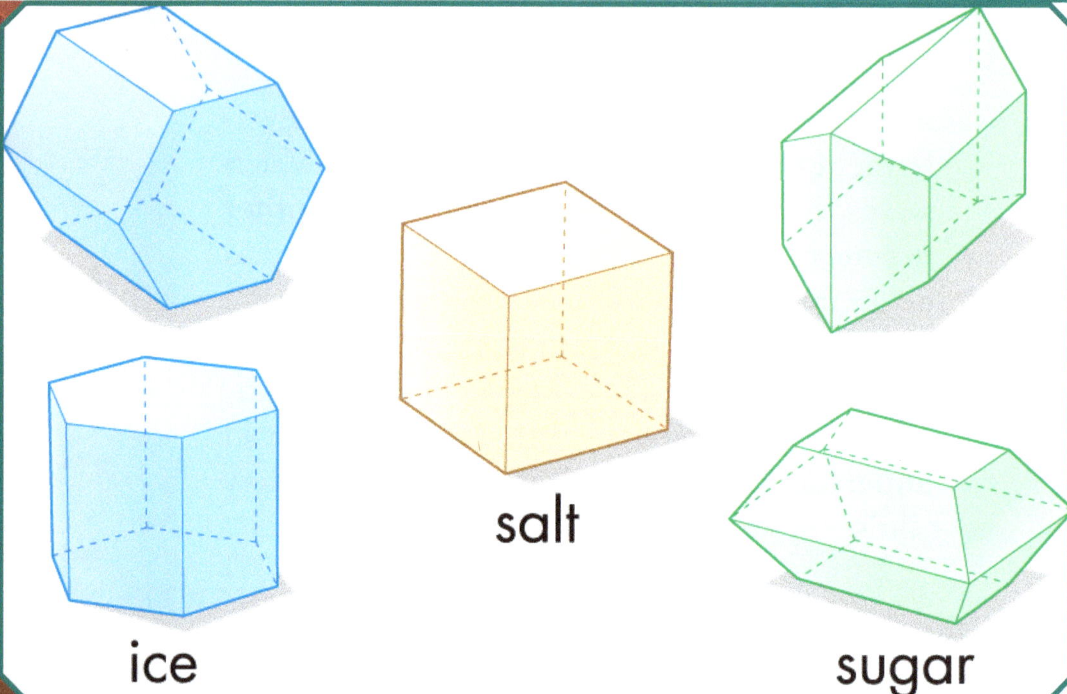

Häuy's studies on crystallography determined that differences in the shapes of crystals reflected differences in their molecular structure. Illustrated above are three common crystals and their external shapes.

In 1814, Jöns Jacob Berzelius of Sweden published a system of mineralogy that offered a comprehensive classification of minerals based on their chemistry. Berzelius recognized the mineral silica as an acid and introduced into mineralogy the group known as silicates. At mid-century, the American geologist James Dwight Dana's *System of Mineralogy*, in its third edition, was reorganized around a chemical classification, which became standard for handbooks.

The development of the polarizing microscope and the technique for grinding sections of rocks so thin as to be virtually transparent came in 1827 from studies of fossilized wood by William Nicol. In 1849, Clifton Sorby showed that minerals viewed in thin section could be identified by their visual properties. Soon afterward, improved classifications of rocks were made on the basis of the minerals that make them up. The German geologist Ferdinand Zirkel's *Mikroscopische Beschaffenheit der Mineralien und Gesteine* (1873; The microscopic nature of minerals and rocks) contains one of the first mineralogical classifications of rocks; it marks the emergence of microscopic petrography—the classification of rocks based on the study of their appearance under a microscope—as an established branch of science.

William Smith and Faunal Succession

In 1683, the zoologist Martin Lister proposed to the Royal Society that a new sort of map be drawn showing the distribution of the different kinds of British "soiles" (vegetable soils and underlying bedrock). Such a work

William Smith

proposed was not accomplished until 132 years later, when William Smith published his *Geologic Map of England and Wales with Part of Scotland* (1815). A self-educated surveyor and engineer, Smith had the habit of collecting fossils and making careful note of the strata that contained them. He discovered that the different strata in England contained distinct groupings of fossils. His map, reproduced on a scale of five miles to the inch, showed twenty different rock units. Smith applied local names in common use to these units—for example, London Clay and Purbeck Beds.

In 1816, Smith published a companion work, *Strata Identified by Organized Fossils*. In it, the organic remains characteristic of each of Smith's rock units were illustrated. His generalization that each formation is "possessed of properties peculiar to itself [and] has the same organized fossils throughout

The Royal Society

Founded in 1660, the Royal Society is the oldest scientific society in Great Britain and one of the oldest in Europe. It began earlier with small, informal groups that met periodically to discuss scientific subjects. The so-called Invisible College of London and Oxford, which first met in 1645, and a number of small academies in England became incorporated in 1662 when the newly restored king, Charles II, granted a charter to the Royal Society of London for the Promotion of Natural Knowledge. Largely composed of Puritan sympathizers and adherents of Francis Bacon, the Royal Society received little more than moral support from the crown, unlike academies on the European continent, which were established by the state and whose members gained an income but lost their independence. From its inception, the society counted important scientists, philosophers, and other intellectual figures among its rank. The stimulus of free expression provided an impetus to scientific thought and developments in England. By the eighteenth century, the achievements of the Royal Society were internationally famous.

Members of the Royal Society are known as fellows. Candidates for membership must be recommended by several fellows who personally attest to the candidate's scientific achievement. The society also has a number of foreign members. In the early twenty-first century, the Royal Society included approximately 1,300 fellows and 130 foreign members.

its course" is the first clear statement of the principle of faunal sequence—that is, that groupings of fossil plants and animals follow or succeed each other in time in a predictable manner. This law of faunal succession is the basis for worldwide correlation of the fossils found in strata into a coherent system. Smith thus demonstrated two kinds of order in nature: order in the spatial arrangement of rock units and order in the succession of ancient forms of life.

Smith's law of faunal succession was another way of saying that there are breaks in the

Using Smith's law of faunal succession, geologists can use fossils to establish the ages of rock layers. In this diagram, sections A and B represent rock layers 200 miles (322 km) apart. Their ages can be established by comparing the fossils in each layer.

sequences of fossilized plants and animals. These breaks were interpreted in two ways: as indicators of some historical episode in which many life forms were destroyed or as evidence for the incompleteness of the fossil record.

Baron Georges Cuvier of France was one of the more distinguished members of a large group of naturalists who believed that discontinuities in the fossil record were evidence of sudden and widespread catastrophes, such as earthquakes, volcanic eruptions, major flooding, and so forth. Cuvier's knowledge of anatomy allowed him to reconstruct from fragmented remains the skeletons of large vertebrate animals found at different strata in northern France. From these studies he discovered that the fossils in all but the youngest deposits belonged to species that were extinct. Moreover, these extinct species had definite ranges up and

down in the stratigraphic column. Cuvier inferred that the successive extinctions were the result of convulsions that had caused strata of the continents to be dislocated and folded and the seas to sweep across the continents and just as suddenly subside.

CHARLES LYELL AND UNIFORMITARIANISM

In contrast to Cuvier's doctrine of catastrophism was the theory of uniformitarianism. Proposed by the British geologist Charles Lyell in his *Principles of Geology* (3 vol., 1830–1833), uniformitarianism was based on two propositions: (1) the causes of geologic change include all the causes that have acted from the earliest time; and (2) these causes have always operated at the same average levels of energy. These two propositions add up to what is known as a "steady-state" theory

Charles Lyell

CHARLES LYELL

The science of geology owes an enormous debt of gratitude to Sir Charles Lyell (1797–1875). It was he who, early in the nineteenth century, devised the theories, methods, and principles on which the modern science is based. His major contribution was in showing that all features of Earth's surface were produced by natural forces operating for long periods of time. His strong arguments that Earth's crust was the product of thousands of millions of years of activity did away with the need for unscientific explanations based on the biblical record or on intermittent natural catastrophes. Lyell's achievements in geology also laid the foundations for evolutionary biology, a field that was to be more fully developed by a young friend, Charles Darwin.

Charles Lyell was born in eastern Scotland on Nov. 14, 1797, and raised near Southampton, England. He graduated from Oxford University in 1819 and went on to study law in London. He had, however, become an amateur geologist, and as the years passed he devoted more and more time to this pursuit. He made explorations in the British Isles, continental Europe, and in the United States. In 1830 the first volume of his *Principles of Geology* was published. Eight years later he published *Elements of Geology.* Both works were hailed as pioneering studies by other scientists, and he was recognized as one of the most eminent scholars in his field. In 1848 he was knighted.

With the publication of Darwin's *Origin of Species* in 1859, the work of Lyell was overshadowed—even among his colleagues. Yet it was to Lyell that Darwin owed much of the information that was the basis of his own work. Lyell continued his studies and revisions of his books until his death in London on Feb. 22, 1875. He was buried in Westminster Abbey.

of Earth. Changes in climate have fluctuated around an average, reflecting changes in the position of land and sea. Progress through time in the organic world is likewise an illusion, the effect of an imperfect fossil record. The main part of the *Principles* was devoted less to theory than to procedures for inferring events from rocks. For his clear exposition of methodology Lyell's work was highly regarded throughout its many editions.

Louis Agassiz and the Ice Age

Huge boulders of granite resting upon limestone of the Jura Mountains in Switzerland were subjects of controversy in the eighteenth and early nineteenth centuries. The Swiss geologist Horace Saussure described these in 1779 and called them erratics. He concluded that they had been swept to their present positions by forceful waters. Saussure's interpretation was in line with the tenets of diluvial geologists, who interpreted erratics and other out-of-place sediment spread over the northern parts of Europe and North America as the work of the biblical flood.

In 1837, the Swiss paleontologist Louis Agassiz proposed that, during a geologically recent

Agassiz suggested that glacial erratics, such as this one near Austwick, England, were evidence that glacial ice had been more expansive in the past, covering much of northern Europe and Asia.

stage of cooling, glacial ice had covered Europe and Asia from the North Pole to the shores of the Mediterranean and Caspian seas. Wherever erratics, till, and striated (scratched or grooved) rock occur, Agassiz claimed evidence exists of this recent catastrophe. Agassiz's theory was not well received at the time. Nonetheless, he began intensive field studies.

In 1840 he published *Études sur les glaciers* (Studies of glaciers). In it, he demonstrated that Alpine glaciers had been far more extensive in the past. That same year, he visited the

LOUIS AGASSIZ

The celebrated Swiss-American naturalist Louis Agassiz (1807–1873) made revolutionary contributions to the study of natural science with landmark work on glacier activity and extinct fishes. He achieved lasting fame through his innovative teaching methods, which altered the character of natural science education in the United States.

Jean Louis Rodolphe Agassiz was born May 28, 1807, in the Swiss village of Môtiers, near Lake Neuchâtel. As a young man, Agassiz studied medicine at the universities of Zurich, Heidelberg, and Munich. His greatest enthusiasm, however, was for zoology. He extensively studied fishes—not only living specimens but also fossil fishes. This led to an interest in geology. His research during a summer spent in a hut on the edge of a glacier helped establish the theory that at different times the greater part of Europe and other northern continents had been covered by vast sheets of ice.

Agassiz became professor of natural history at Neuchâtel in 1832. He remained there until 1846, when he came to America to deliver a series of lectures in Boston. In 1848, he accepted the chair of natural history at Harvard University and lived in America until the end of his life.

Agassiz wrote extensively, delivered popular lectures on scientific subjects, and engaged in expeditions in various parts of the United States and Brazil. He was the first director of the Museum of Comparative Zoology at Harvard, often called the Agassiz Museum. When urged to turn his great scientific knowledge to financial profit, he impatiently replied that he "had no time to make money."

A few months before his death, Agassiz established a summer school of science on the island of Penikese in Buzzards Bay, off the southeast coast of Massachusetts. This was the first school for studying science directly from specimens and in close contact with nature. Agassiz died at Cambridge in 1873. On his grave were placed a boulder that came from the glacier near the spot where his hut once stood and pine trees sent from his old home in Switzerland.

British Isles and extended the glacial doctrine to Scotland, northern England, and Ireland. In 1846, he carried his campaign to North America and there found additional evidence for an ice age.

GEOLOGIC TIME AND THE AGE OF THE EARTH

By mid-century, fossil-containing strata of Europe had been grouped into systems arranged in chronological order. By using the principles of superposition and faunal succession, these systems could be compiled to form the stratigraphic column. The time elapsed during the formation of a system became known as a period. In turn, the periods were grouped into geologic eras:

the Paleozoic (Cambrian through Permian periods), Mesozoic (Triassic, Jurassic, and Cretaceous periods), and Cenozoic (Paleogene, Neogene, and Quaternary periods).

Charles Darwin's *Origin of Species* (1859) offered a theoretical explanation for the principle of faunal sequence. The fossils of the successive systems are different not only

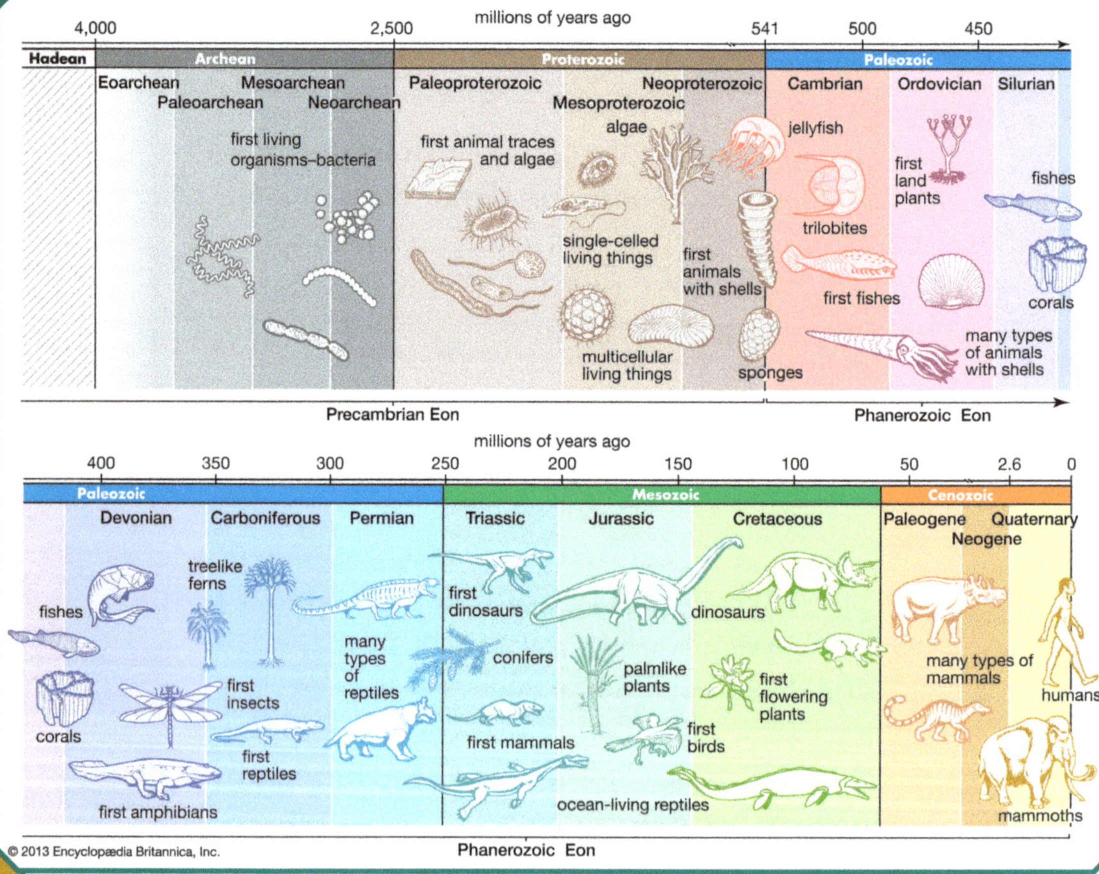

Darwin offered the first acceptable explanation for the differences in life forms discovered in different rock layers. His theory of evolution by natural selection explained why older life forms had been small and simple, whereas later forms were more complex and varied.

because parts of the stratigraphic record are missing but also because most species have lost in their struggles for survival. Furthermore, those that do survive evolve into new forms over time. Darwin borrowed two ideas from Lyell and the uniformitarians: that geologic time is virtually without limit, and that a series of minor changes over long periods of time produce remarkable changes in natural beings.

Beginning in 1864, William Thomson (later Lord Kelvin) attacked Lyell's steady-state theory of Earth and placed limits on the length of geologic time. Earth might function as a heat machine, but it could not also be a perpetual motion machine. Assuming that Earth was originally molten, Thomson calculated that Earth had to have first become a solid body between 20 million and 400 million years ago.

Other physicists of note put even narrower limits on Earth's age. These ranged down to 15 million or 20 million years. All these calculations, however, were based on the common assumption that Earth's substance was inert and thus cannot generate new heat. Shortly before the end of the nineteenth century, this assumption was negated by the discovery of radioactive elements that disintegrate spontaneously and release heat to Earth in the process.

CONCEPTS OF LANDFORM EVOLUTION

The scientific exploration of the American West after the Civil War yielded much new information on the sculpture of the landscape by streams. In 1875–1876, John Wesley Powell explained how streams may come to flow across mountain ranges rather than detour around them. The Green River does not follow some structural crack in its gorge across the Uinta Mountains; instead it has cut its canyon as the mountain range was slowly bowed up. Given enough time, streams will erode their drainage basins to plains approaching sea level as a base.

Grove Karl Gilbert's *Report on the Geology of the Henry Mountains* (1877) offered a detailed analysis of how streams function. According to Gilbert, all streams work toward a state of dynamic equilibrium, when the net effect of the flowing water is neither erosion of the bed nor deposition of sediment.

After 1884, William Morris Davis developed the concept of the geomorphic cycle. During this cycle, elevated regions pass through stages of dissection (by water sources) and denudation (being made bare by erosion), characterized as youthful, mature, and old. Youthful landscapes have broad mountains or hills and

William Morris Davis

narrow valleys. With further denudation, the original surface on which the streams began their work is reduced to ridgetops. Finally, in the stage of old age, the region is reduced to a nearly featureless plain near sea level. During any of these stages, elevation of the region will activate a new cycle. Davis's views dominated thought on how landscapes change until well into the twentieth century, when approaches based on data measurement resulted in the rediscovery of Gilbert's ideas.

GRAVITY, ISOSTASY, AND EARTH'S FIGURE

Discoveries of regional differences in Earth's gravity led to the realization that high mountain ranges have reduced masses about equal to the apparent surface loads represented by the mountains' size.

In the eighteenth century, the French scientist Pierre Bouguer observed that the movements of a pendulum off its direct trajectory in a straight line in Peru were much shorter than they should be if the Andes represented a load placed on top of Earth's crust. Similar discoveries were later found along the Himalayan front. To explain these strange observations, it was necessary to assume that beneath some depth within Earth, pressures are hydrostatic (equal on all sides). If heavier loads are placed on top of the crust, the crust will sink to compensate for the additional mass. It will rise again when the load is removed. In 1899, Clarence Edward Dutton of the United States called this tendency toward general equilibrium maintained through the rising and lowering of Earth's crust isostasy.

Evidence for vertical movements of the crust was supplied by studies of Earth's strata in different regions. In 1883, another American geologist, James Hall, had demonstrated that Paleozoic rocks of the folded Appalachians were several times as thick as geologic sequences of the same age in the plateaus and plains to the west. He concluded that the folded strata in the mountains must have built up in a linear underwater trough that filled with sediment as it disappeared.

HYDROLOGIC SCIENCES

In the nineteenth century, significant advances were made in the mathematical study of water and its discharge. Such advances occurred both in Europe, where engineers sought to understand the flow of groundwater, and in the United States, where exploration of the

Mississippi River and the vast territorial acquisitions made beyond it spurred on a greater interest in the study of streams.

The other notable development in hydrology in the nineteenth century was an increased interest in the deep sea and tides, arising in part from the expansion of telegraphic cables and also from the notable voyages of the *Beagle* and the *Challenger*.

DARCY'S LAW

Studies measuring the movement of water in streams and aquifers led to mathematical formulas relating water discharge to other factors. The French engineer Henri-Philibert-Gaspard Darcy was the first to state clearly a law describing the flow of groundwater. He reported his experiments in 1856. They were based on the ideas that an aquifer worked as a main line that connected two water reservoirs at different levels and that an artesian well was like a pipe drawing water from a main line under pressure. His investigations of water flow through stratified beds of sand led him to conclude that the rate of flow is directly proportional to the energy loss and inversely proportional to the length of the path of flow.

Another French engineer, Arsène-Jules-Étienne-Juvénal Dupuit, extended Darcy's work. Dupuit developed equations for underground flow toward a well, for the recharge of aquifers, and for the discharge of artesian wells. The Austrian hydrologist Philip Forchheimer introduced a theory to

Henri Darcy

Henri-Philibert-Gaspard Darcy (1803–1858) was a French hydraulic engineer who first derived the equation that describes the flow of water through an aquifer. This expression is known as Darcy's law.

After receiving a degree in civil engineering from the L'École des Ponts et Chaussées (School of Bridges and Roads) in Paris, Darcy returned to his native city of Dijon, where he was entrusted with the design and construction of the municipal water supply system. During the course of this work, he conducted experiments on pipe flow and demonstrated that resistance to flow depended on the surface roughness of the pipe material, which previously had not been considered a factor. Planning to use the technique of water purification by filtration through sand, he also studied cases in which the pipe was filled with sand. From the data gathered, he derived the law that bears his name. Darcy's law forms the quantitative basis of a wide range of scientific discipline, from hydrogeology to petroleum engineering.

analyze the flow by gravity of underground water toward wells. Furthermore he developed equations for determining the critical distance between a river and a well beyond which water from the river will not move into the well.

SURFACE WATER DISCHARGE

The studies of Andrew Atkinson Humphreys and Henry Larcom Abbot during the Mississippi Delta Survey of 1851–1860 resulted in a complicated formula for the discharge of streams. Their formula contained no term for the roughness of a water channel. On this and other grounds, it was later found to be inapplicable to the fast flowing streams of mountain regions. In 1869, Emile-Oscar Ganguillet and Rudolph Kutter developed a more applicable discharge equation based on their studies of flow in Swiss mountain streams.

Toward the end of the nineteenth century, systematic studies of the discharge of streams had become common. In the United States, the Geological Survey, following its establishment in 1879, became the main agency for collecting and publishing data on water discharge. By 1906, stream gauging was conducted nationwide.

Foundations of Oceanography

In 1807, Thomas Jefferson ordered the establishment of the US Coast Survey (today known as the National Ocean Survey). Modeled after British and French agencies founded in the 1700s, the agency was charged with the responsibilities of surveying water and land, studies of tides, and preparation of charts.

Beginning in 1842, the US Navy undertook expansive oceanographic operations through its office of charts and instruments. Lieutenant Matthew Fontaine Maury promoted international cooperation in gathering weather and hydrologic data at sea. In 1847, Maury compiled the first wind and current charts for the North Atlantic. In 1854, he issued the first depth map to 4,000 fathoms (7,300 meters). His *Physical Geography of the Sea* (1855) is generally considered the first textbook of oceanography.

The voyage of the *Beagle* (1831–1836) is remembered for Darwin's contributions to the biological and geologic sciences. From his observations in the South Pacific, Darwin formulated a theory for the origin of coral reefs, which is still accepted today with only minor changes. He viewed different types of coral reefs as successive stages in a sequence of development.

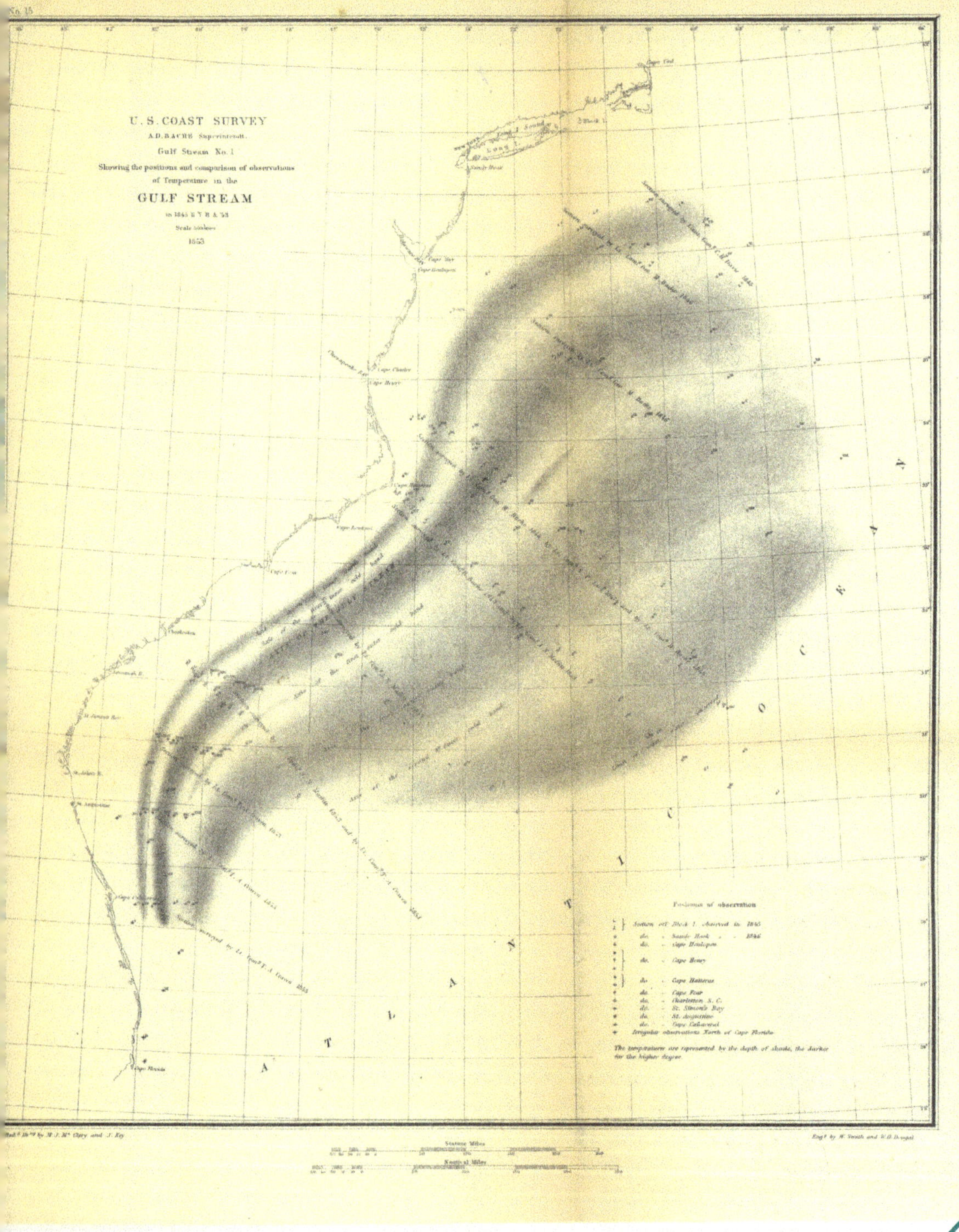

A US Coast Survey map shows the positions of recorded temperatures in the Gulf Stream in 1845–1848 and in 1853.

The volcanic islands around which reef-building organisms are attached slowly sink; at the same time the shallow-water organisms that form the reefs build their colonies upward so as to remain in the sunlit layers of water. As the island sinks under water, what began as a fringing reef surrounding a landmass becomes an atoll—a ringlike island made of coral.

Laying telegraphic cables across the Atlantic required investigations of the ocean floor, of deep-sea currents, and of the deep-sea animals that might damage the cables. British explorations in 1868 and 1869 turned up surprising information about the ocean. Soon after these voyages, the *Challenger* was sent out to determine "the conditions of the Deep Sea throughout the Great Ocean Basins."

The *Challenger* left port in December 1872 and returned in May 1876. In that lapse, the ship logged 68,890 nautical miles (127,600 kilometers) and occupied 350 stations in all oceans except the Arctic. The work involved in analyzing the information gathered during the expedition was completed by Sir John Murray, and the results filled fifty large volumes. Hundreds of new species of marine organisms were described, including new forms of life from deep waters. The temperature of water at the bottom of the oceans was found to be nearly constant below the 2,000-fathom level, averaging about 36.5°F (2.5°C) in the North Atlantic and 35°F (2°C) in the North Pacific. The expedition found wide variations in depths of water; from the dredgings of the ocean floor came new types of sediment—red clay as well as oozes made up of the minute skeletons of several forms of ocean life. Improved charts of the principal surface currents were produced, and the precise location of many oceanic islands was determined for the first time. Seventy-seven samples of seawater were taken at different stations from depths ranging downward to about 4,921 feet (1.5 kilometers). The German-born chemist Wilhelm Dittmar measured the levels of the seven major constituents (other than the hydrogen and oxygen of the water itself)—namely, sodium, calcium, magnesium, potassium, chloride, bromide, and sulfate. Surprisingly, the percentages of these components turned out to be nearly the same in all samples.

Efforts to analyze the rise and fall of the tides in mathematical terms—and thus to predict the tides at specific locations—has never been wholly successful. This is because of local variations in configuration of shore and seafloor. Nevertheless, harmonic tidal analysis gives vital first approximations that are essential to tidal

From December 1872 through May 1876, the HMS *Challenger* explored deep-sea conditions in all of Earth's oceans except the Arctic.

prediction. In 1884, William Ferrel of the US Coast and Geodetic Survey invented a mechanical analog tidal prediction device. Improved models of Ferrel's device were used until 1965, when the work of the analog machines was taken over by electronic computers.

Atmospheric Sciences

The atmospheric sciences made vast improvements in the understanding of weather throughout the nineteenth century. A greater understanding of air pressure and its relationship to storm patterns informed advanced tracking of weather systems, a logical precursor to attempts to forecast the weather. The development of cloud classifications and various kinds of weather maps further advanced the field of meteorology (the study of weather).

COMPOSITION OF THE ATMOSPHERE

Studies of barometric pressure by the British chemist and physicist John Dalton led him to conclude that evaporation and condensation of vapor do not involve chemical transformations. The introduction of vapor into the air by evaporation must change the average specific gravity of the air column and, without altering the height of that column, will change the reading of the barometer. In 1857, Rudolf Clausius, a German physicist, clarified the mechanics of evaporation in his kinetic theory of gases. Evaporation occurs when more molecules of a liquid are leaving its surface than returning to it. Also, the higher the temperature, the more of these escaped molecules will be in space at any one time.

Following the invention of the hot-air balloon by the Montgolfier brothers in 1783, balloonists produced some useful information on the atmosphere and its composition. In 1804, the French chemist Joseph-Louis Gay-Lussac ascended to about 22,966 feet (7,000 meters) and took samples of air. He later determined that the rarefied—or less dense—air at that altitude contained the same percentage of oxygen (21.49 percent) as the air on the ground. In 1874, Austrian meteorologist Julius von Hann, interpreting data from balloon trips and climbing the Alps and Himalayas, concluded that about 90 percent of all the water vapor in the atmosphere is concentrated below 19,685 feet (6,000 meters). It thus follows that high mountains can be barriers against the transport of water vapor.

UNDERSTANDING OF CLOUDS, FOG, AND DEW

Most of the names given to clouds (cirrus, cumulus, stratus, nimbus, and their combinations) were coined in 1803 by the English meteorologist Luke Howard. Howard's effort was not simply to categorize clouds; he recognized that, in their shapes and changing forms, clouds reflect "the general causes which effect all the variations of the atmosphere."

After Otto von Guericke's experiments, it was widely believed that water vapor condenses into cloud as soon as the air containing

In 1803, the English meteorologist Luke Howard named and classified the various types of clouds, as shown in the above illustration.

it cools to the dew point. That this is not necessarily so was demonstrated by Paul-Jean Coulier of France from experiments reported in 1875. Coulier found that the sudden expansion of air in glass flasks failed to produce an artificial cloud if the air in the system was filtered through cotton wool. He concluded that dust in the air was essential to the formation of cloud in the flask.

Starting in the 1820s, efforts were made to classify precipitation based on causes behind the lowering of temperature. In 1841, the American astronomer-meteorologist Elias Loomis recognized the following causes: warm air coming into contact with cold earth or water, which forms fog; mixing of warm and cold air currents, which commonly results in light rains; and sudden transport of air into high regions, such as air flow up a mountain slope or by warm air currents riding over an opposing current of cold air, which may produce heavy rains.

Observation and Study of Storms

Storms, particularly tropical revolving storms, were subjects of much interest. As early as 1697, some of the more spectacular features of hurricanes and typhoons were recorded in William Dampier's *New Voyage Round the World*. On July 4, 1687, Dampier's ship survived the passage of what he called a "tuffoon" off the coast of China. The captain's vivid account of this experience clearly describes the calm central eye of the storm and the passage of winds from opposite directions as the storm moved past. In 1828, Heinrich Wilhelm Dove, a Prussian meteorologist, recognized that tropical revolving storms are traveling systems with strong winds moving counterclockwise in the Northern Hemisphere and clockwise in the Southern Hemisphere.

The whirlwind character of these storms was independently established by the American meteorologist William C. Redfield in the case of the September hurricane that struck New England in 1821. He noted that in central Connecticut, the trees had been toppled toward the northwest, whereas some fifty miles (eighty kilometers) to the west, they had fallen in the opposite direction. Redfield identified the belt between the equator and the tropics as the region in which hurricanes are generated, and he recognized how the tracks of these storms tend

"Supertyphoon" Chaba *(right)* approaching Japan and Typhoon Aere *(left)* hitting Taiwan, as photographed by the GOES-9 satellite, Aug. 25, 2004.

to veer toward the east when they enter the belt of westerly winds at about latitude 30°N.

In 1849, Sir William Reid, a British meteorologist and military engineer, studied the revolving storms that occur south of the equator in the Indian Ocean and confirmed that they have reversed rotations and curvatures of path compared with those of the Northern Hemisphere. Captain Henry Piddington subsequently investigated revolving storms affecting the Bay of Bengal and Arabian Sea, and in 1855, he named these cyclones in his *Sailor's Horn-book for the Laws of Storms in all Parts of the World*.

Beginning in 1835, James Pollard Espy, an American meteorologist, began extensive studies of storms from which he developed a theory to explain their sources of energy. Radially convergent winds, he believed, cause the air to rise in their area of collision. Upward movement of moist air is attended by condensation and precipitation. Latent heat released through the change of vapor to cloud or water causes further expansion and rising of the air. The higher the moist air rises, the more the equilibrium of the system is disturbed, and this equilibrium cannot be restored until moist air at the surface ceases to flow toward the ascending column.

That radially convergent winds are not necessary to the rising of large air masses was demonstrated by Loomis in the case of a great storm that passed across the northeastern United States in December 1836. From his studies of wind patterns, changes of temperature, and changes in barometric pressure, he concluded that a cold northwest wind had displaced a wind blowing from the southeast by flowing under it. The southeast wind made its escape by ascending from Earth's surface. Loomis had recognized what today would be called a frontal surface.

WEATHER AND CLIMATE

Modern meteorology began when the electromagnetic telegraph made it possible to create the daily weather map, which was then used to analyze and predict the weather. In the United States, the first telegraph line was strung in 1844 between Washington, DC, and Baltimore. As telegraphic networks were expanded, the physicist Joseph Henry arranged for telegraph companies to have meteorological instruments in exchange for current data on weather telegraphed to the Smithsonian Institution. About 500 stations joined this effort by 1860. The American

Civil War temporarily prevented expanding the network.

Meanwhile, a different disaster accelerated development of large-scale meteorology in Europe. On Nov. 14, 1854, an unexpected storm wrecked British and French warships in the Black Sea. Had word of the approaching storm been telegraphed to the nearest port, the ships might have been saved. This incident led to the establishment of a national storm-warning service in France in 1856. In 1863, the Paris Observatory started publishing the first weather maps in modern format.

In 1871, the first national weather service in the United States began operations as an agency of the Department of War. Its initial goal was to provide storm warnings for the eastern coasts and the Great Lakes. In 1877, forecasts of temperature changes and precipitation were, on average, 74 percent accurate. Cold-wave forecasts were 79 percent accurate. After 1878, daily weather maps were published.

Synoptic, or large-scale, meteorology made it possible to track storm systems over wide areas. In 1868, the British meteorologist Alexander Buchan published a map showing the path of a cyclonic depression across North America, the Atlantic, and into northern Europe.

Buchan's study marks the beginning of modern meteorology.

In addition to weather maps, other kinds of maps showing regional variations in weather

WEATHER MAPS

A weather map is any map or chart that shows the meteorological elements at a given time over an extended area. The earliest weather charts were made by collecting weather reports by mail. However, in 1816, the German physicist Heinrich Wilhelm Brandes created the first weather maps, which were hand drawn and reconstructed from data collected in 1783. The first telegraphic collection of synoptic weather reports and their mapping for forecasting was accomplished by Urbain-J.-J. Le Verrier during the mid-1800s.

The most common type of surface weather map, normally issued by a central weather office, shows the distribution of surface isobars (lines of constant pressure) and the location of fronts and severe weather areas such as hurricanes and other storms. At many locations on the map a standard plotting code indicates wind direction and speed, air temperature and dew point, barometric pressure and its change during the preceding hours, the amount and types of clouds, the weather type (including restrictions to visibility), and the amount and type of precipitation. In the United States, weather maps are issued every three hours by the National Weather Service. When used in conjunction with charts showing the upper-air flow pattern at 850, 700, 500, 300, and 200 millibars of atmospheric pressure and with satellite photographs of the distribution of clouds, these maps are valuable forecasting tools.

and climate were produced. In 1817, Alexander von Humboldt published a map showing the distribution of average annual temperatures over most of the Northern Hemisphere. Humboldt was the first to use isothermal lines—lines connecting areas with equal average temperatures—in mapping temperature.

In 1869, Buchan published the first maps of average monthly and annual pressure for the entire world. In 1886, Léon-Philippe Teisserenc de Bort of France published maps showing average annual cloudiness

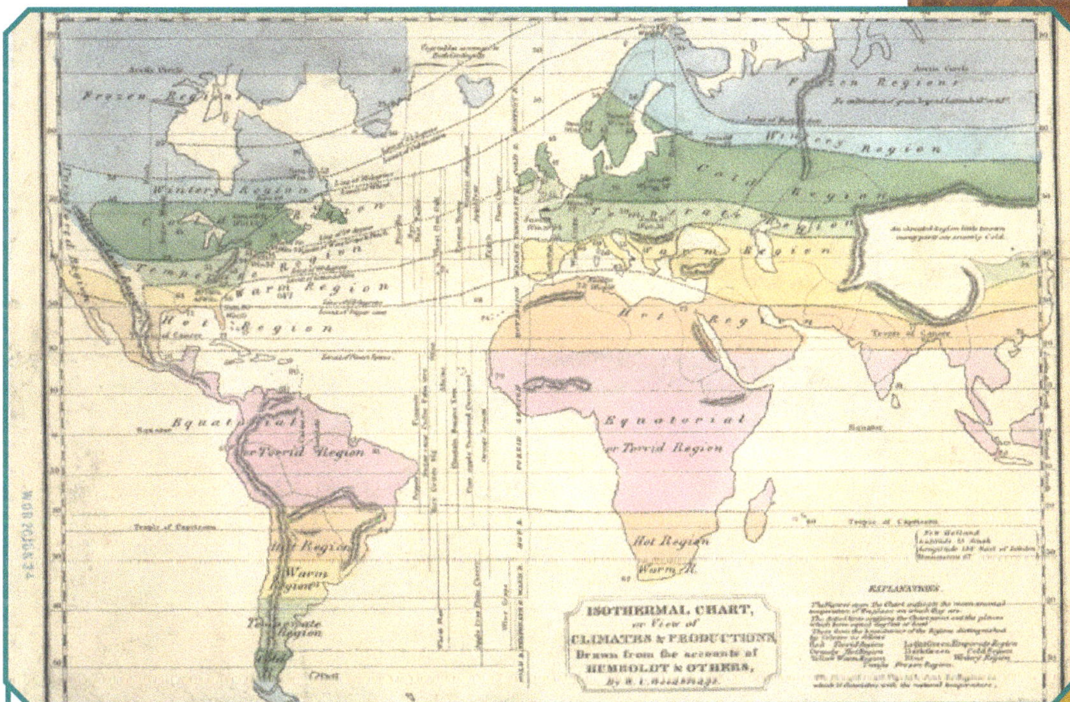

This isothermal chart published in 1823 by Alexander von Humboldt uses lines to connect different regions on the map with equal average temperatures.

over Earth for each month and the year. In 1882, Loomis published the first world map of precipitation showing average annual precipitation by isohyets—lines connecting areas with equal average rainfall. In 1899, the British cartographer Andrew John Herbertson further refined this work with maps that showed precipitation for each month of the year.

CHAPTER 4

THE 20TH CENTURY TO THE PRESENT: MODERN TRENDS AND DEVELOPMENTS

Since the early twentieth century, the earth sciences have been marked across the board by rapid developments in the equipment and technology at hand to conduct research. This is thanks, in large part, to the advent of digitized equipment. Furthermore, humans' improved ability to bore into Earth, to collect data from below the ocean floor, and to travel into the upper atmosphere and beyond has enabled the collection of data and observations previously inaccessible to humans.

An improved understanding of Earth's history and functioning becomes increasingly crucial to developing a forecast for future natural events that will reshape Earth and impact humanity.

GEOLOGIC SCIENCES

The development of the geologic sciences in the modern day has been influenced by two major "revolutions." The first involved technological advances that resulted in much improved instrumentation, the prime examples being the many types of sophisticated computerized devices. The second centered on the development of plate tectonics theory, the most profound and influential conceptual advance the earth sciences have ever known.

RADIOMETRIC DATING

In 1905, shortly after the discovery of radioactivity, the American chemist Bertram Boltwood suggested that lead is one of the disintegration products of uranium. If true, then the older a uranium-bearing mineral was the greater its proportional part of lead would be. By analyzing specimens whose relative geologic ages were known, Boltwood found that the ratio of lead to uranium did increase with age. After estimating the rate of this radioactive change, he calculated that the absolute ages of his specimens ranged from 410 million to 2.2 billion years. Though his figures were too high by about 20 percent, they were large

Bertram Boltwood

Bertram Borden Boltwood (1870–1927) was an American chemist and physicist whose work on the radioactive decay of uranium and thorium was important in the development of the theory of isotopes.

In 1904, Boltwood showed that many of the radioactive elements decay into other radioactive elements. He discovered ionium, now called thorium-230. In 1905, he proposed that lead is the final decay product of uranium. Two years later, he developed a method of determining the age of some rocks by measuring the ratio of lead and uranium. Additional methods of radiometric dating that followed greatly altered estimates of the age of Earth and proved invaluable in archaeology.

enough to dispose of the short scale of geologic time proposed by Lord Kelvin.

The mass spectrometer separates the different isotopes of the same element, and it can measure the variations in these amounts of isotopes to within one part in 10,000. Versions of the modern device were invented in the early 1920s and 1930s. It was during World War II, however, that the device was improved substantially to help develop the atomic bomb. Soon after the war, the mass spectrometer was first applied to the study of geochronology—the study of the past as informed by geology. By determining the amount of the parent and daughter isotopes present in a sample and by knowing their rate of radioactive decay, the age of the sample can be calculated.

For dating minerals and rocks, investigators commonly use the following couplets of parent and daughter isotopes: thorium-232–lead-208, uranium-235–lead-207, samarium-147–neodymium-143, rubidium-87–strontium-87, potassium-40–argon-40, and argon-40–argon-39. An instrument called the SHRIMP (Sensitive High Resolution Ion Microprobe) allows for the accurate determination of the uranium-lead age of the mineral zircon, which has revolutionized our understanding of when zircon-bearing igneous granite rocks first formed. Another technological development is the ICP-MS (Inductively Coupled Plasma Mass Spectrometer). This device can provide the isotopic age of the minerals zircon, titanite, rutile, and monazite. These minerals are common to many igneous and metamorphic rocks.

Such techniques have had a huge impact on scientific knowledge of Earth history. With them, precise dates can be obtained on rocks in all mountain belts ranging from the early

A rock formation called "faux amphibolite," from the Nuvvuagittuq greenstone belt in northern Quebec, dated to 4.28 billion years ago.

Archean (about 4 billion years old) to the early Neogene (roughly 20 million years old) periods. The oldest known rocks on Earth are estimated to be more than 4 billion years old. Scientists can also work backward to estimate a figure of about 4.6 billion years is for the minimum age of Earth. This figure is of the same order as ages obtained for certain meteorites and lunar rocks.

Experimental Study of Rocks

Experimental petrology, the study of rocks, began with the work of the chemist Jacobus Henricus van 't Hoff. Between 1896 and 1908, he clarified the complex sequence of chemical reactions involved in the precipitation of salts from evaporated seawater. Van 't Hoff aimed to explain the succession of mineral salts present in rocks in Germany from the Permian period. From aqueous solutions he successfully produced artificial minerals and rocks like those found in natural salt deposits.

Van 't Hoff's work stimulated studies of the minerals that crystallized from silicate melts, which simulated the magmas that igneous rocks formed from. The Canadian petrologist Norman L. Bowen conducted extensive studies of silicate systems that were published in his *Evolution of the Igneous Rocks* (1928).

Experimental petrology, both at the low-temperature range explored by van 't Hoff and in the high ranges of temperature investigated by Bowen, continues to provide laboratory evidence for interpreting the chemical history of rocks. Experimental petrology also provides valuable data on individual minerals and of the reactions between different minerals in a wide variety of chemical systems. These experiments are done at elevated temperatures and pressures that simulate those in the different levels of Earth's crust. This allows the metamorphic petrologist today to compare the minerals found in natural rocks with comparable examples produced in the laboratory under similar pressure and temperature limits.

Another branch of experimental science relates to the deformation of rocks. In 1906, the American physicist P. W. Bridgman developed a technique for subjecting rock samples to high pressures similar to those deep in Earth. Studies of the behavior of rocks in the laboratory have shown that their strength increases with confining pressure but decreases with rise in temperature. Down to depths of a few kilometers, rocks increase in strength due to increasing pressure. However, at greater depths, higher temperatures take effect and cause rocks to flow rather than fracture.

In 1959, two American geologists, Marion King Hubbert and William W. Rubey, demonstrated that fluids in the pores of rock might reduce internal friction and allow the rocks to glide over nearly horizontal planes. More recently, the Norwegian petrologist Hans Ramberg performed many experiments with a large centrifuge that produced a negative gravity effect and thus was able to create structures simulating salt domes, which rise because of the relatively low density of the salt in comparison with that of surrounding rocks.

CRYSTALLOGRAPHY

In the nineteenth century, crystallographers could study only the external form of minerals. However, when the German physicist Wilhelm Conrad Röntgen discovered X-rays in 1895, it became possible to consider the internal structure of minerals. In 1912, another German physicist, Max von Laue, realized that X-rays were scattered and deflected at regular angles when they passed through a copper sulfate crystal. He produced the first X-ray diffraction pattern on a photographic film. A year later the British physicist William Henry

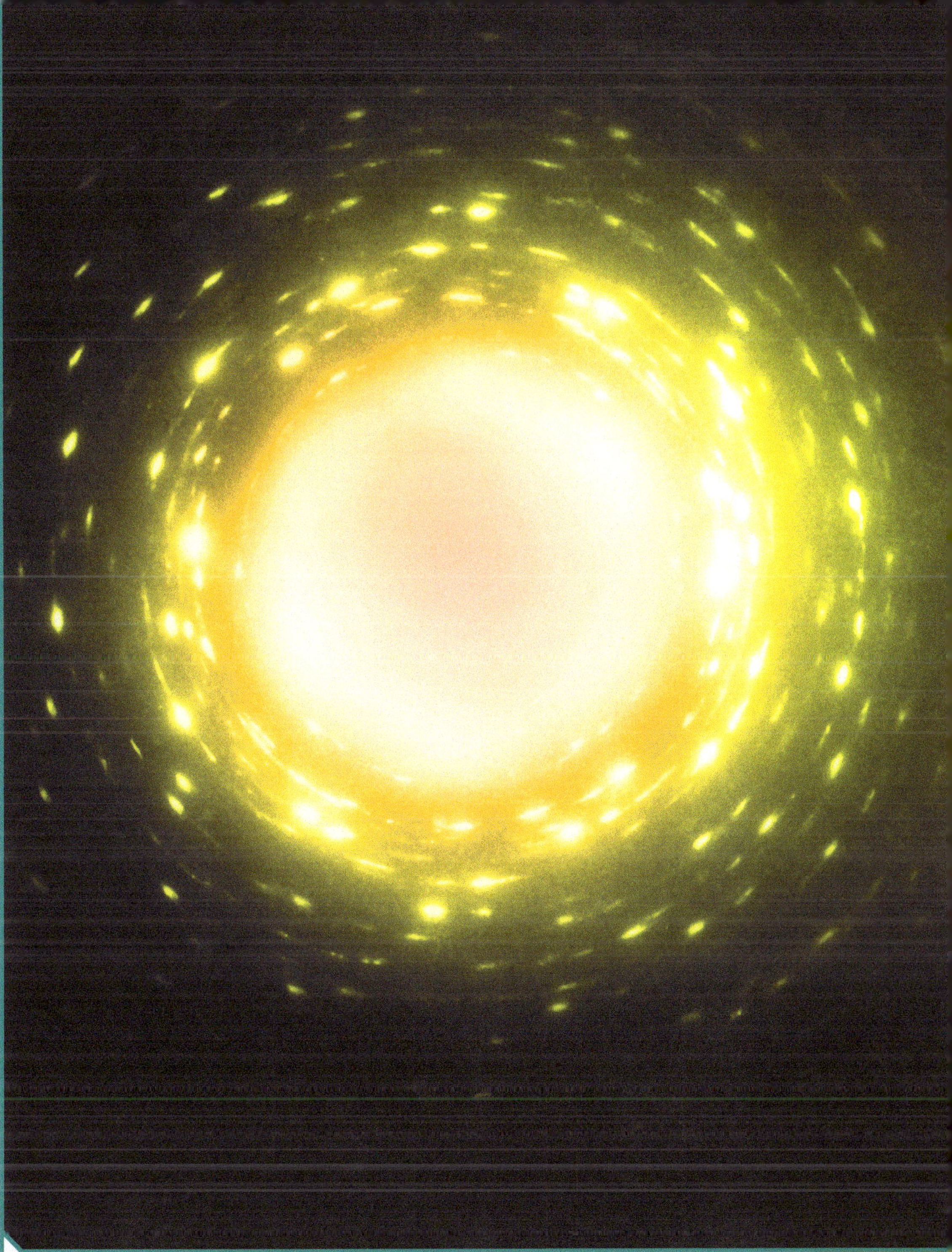

This X-ray diffraction pattern of polyethylene crystals reveals the shape and molecular structure of the crystals that produced it. The diffraction pattern has been color-enhanced.

Bragg observed that such a pattern reflected the layers of atoms in the crystal structure. He succeeded in determining for the first time the atomic crystal structure of the mineral halite (sodium chloride). These discoveries had a long-lasting influence on crystallography because they led to the development of the X-ray powder diffractometer, which is now widely used to identify minerals and to determine their crystal structure.

CHEMICAL ANALYSIS OF ROCKS AND MINERALS

Advanced chemical equipment has greatly changed our understanding of the composition of rocks and minerals. For example, the XRF (X-Ray Fluorescence) spectrometer can measure the major and trace element abundances of many chemical elements in a rock sample down to parts-per-million concentrations. This method has been used to differentiate successive stages of igneous rocks in the plate-tectonic cycle.

The metamorphic petrologist can use the bulk composition of a recrystallized rock to define the structure of the original rock, assuming that no structural change has occurred during the metamorphic process. Next, the electron microprobe bombards a thin microscopic slice of a mineral in a sample with a beam of electrons, which can determine the chemical composition of the mineral almost instantly. This method has wide applications in industrial mineralogy, materials science, igneous geochemistry, and metamorphic petrology.

Micropaleontology

Microscopic fossils, such as ostracods, foraminifera, and pollen grains, are common in sediments of the Mesozoic and Cenozoic eras (from about 252 million years ago to the present). Because the rock chips recovered from oil wells are so small, a high-resolution instrument known as a scanning electron microscope was needed to study the microfossils. The classification of microfossils of organisms that lived within short time spans allowed Mesozoic-Cenozoic sediments to be subdivided in great detail. This technique also had a huge impact on the study of Precambrian life (organisms that existed more than 541 million years ago). Carbon-containing spheroids and filaments about 0.3–0.4 inch (7–10 millimeters) long are recorded in 3.5 billion-year-old sediments in the Pilbara region of northwestern Western

Foraminifera fossils can be seen in this rock sample from the Eocene Epoch, which began 56 million years ago and ended 33.9 million years ago.

Australia and in the lower Onverwacht Series of the Barberton belt in South Africa; these are the oldest reliable records of life on Earth.

SEISMOLOGY AND THE STRUCTURE OF EARTH

Earthquake study was institutionalized in 1880 with the formation of the Seismological Society of Japan under the leadership of John Milne, an English geologist. Milne and his associates invented the first accurate seismographs—devices that measure and record the movement of Earth during an earthquake—including the instrument later known as the Milne seismograph. Seismology has revealed much about the structure of Earth's core, mantle, and crust. The English seismologist Richard Dixon Oldham's studies of earthquake records in 1906 led to the discovery of Earth's core. From studies of the Croatian quake of Oct. 8, 1909, the geophysicist Andrija Mohorovičić discovered the boundary that separates the crust from the underlying mantle.

Today, there are more than 1,000 seismograph stations around the world. Their data is used to compile seismicity maps. These maps show that earthquake epicenters are aligned in narrow, continuous belts along the boundaries of lithospheric plates. (The lithosphere is the outermost layer of the solid Earth.) The earthquake foci (where an earthquake originates)

ANDRIJA MOHOROVIČIĆ

A Croatian meteorologist and geophysicist, Andrija Mohorovičić (1857–1936) discovered the boundary between Earth's crust and mantle.

The son of a shipyard carpenter, Mohorovičić was born in Volosko, Croatia, on Jan. 23, 1857. As a young man, he studied under the physicist and philosopher Ernst Mach at the University of Prague and was graduated in mathematics and physics (1875). In 1892, Mohorovičić became director of the meteorological observatory in Zagreb. As early as 1908, he succeeded in acquiring new and improved seismographic equipment for the observatory, making it one of the most advanced in Europe. The following year, the station recorded a destructive earthquake in the Kulpa Valley. From these readings and those of other stations, Mohorovičić observed that certain seismic waves arrived at detecting stations sooner than anticipated. He deduced that the earthquake was centered in an outer layer of Earth—since called its crust—and that the fast waves had traveled through an inner layer—the mantle. Between them lay what was later named the Mohorovičić discontinuity (or simply, the Moho). Much later observations by more sophisticated instruments confirmed his discovery. Modern instruments have determined that the speeds of seismic waves rapidly increase to more than 5 miles per second (8 kilometers per second) at this boundary.

Mohorovičić later discovered a technique for locating the epicenters of earthquakes and calculated the travel time of seismic waves. He was an early advocate of earthquake-resistant construction.

outline the mid-oceanic ridges in the Atlantic, Pacific, and Indian oceans where the plates separate, while around the margins of the Pacific where the plates converge, they lie in a dipping plane, or Benioff zone.

Since 1950, additional information on the crust has been obtained from the analysis of artificial tremors produced by chemical explosions. These studies have shown that the Moho (the boundary that separates Earth's crust and mantle) is present under all continents at an average depth of 22 miles (35 kilometers) and

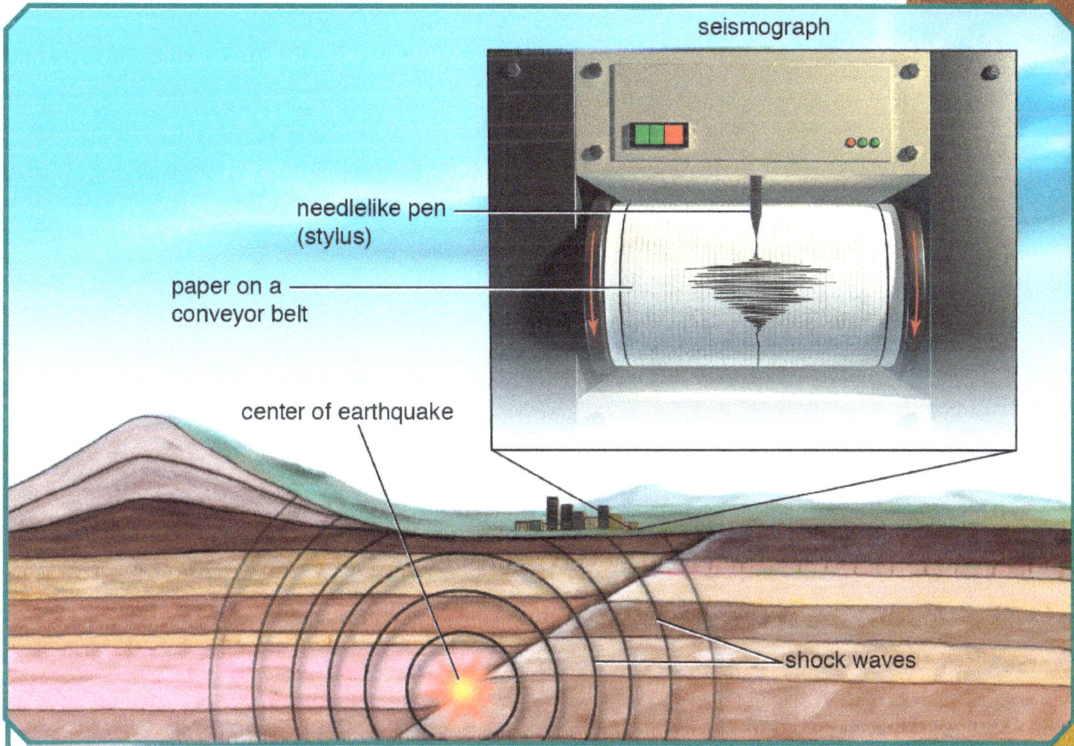

Scientists record the shock waves produced in an earthquake with an instrument called a seismograph. As the machine moves back and forth with the ground, a pen records the movement on a roll of paper.

that the crust above it thickens under young mountain ranges to depths of 43 miles (70 kilometers) in the Andes and the Himalayas. In such investigations the reflections of the seismic waves generated from a series of "shot" points are also recorded, and this makes it possible to construct a profile of the subsurface structure. This is seismic reflection profiling, the main method of exploration used by the oil industry. During the late 1970s, a new technique for generating seismic waves was invented: thumping and vibrating the surface of the ground with a gas-propelled piston from a large truck.

The Theory of Plate Tectonics

Plate tectonics has revolutionized virtually every discipline of the earth sciences since the late 1960s and early 1970s. It has served as a unifying model for explaining geologic phenomena that were formerly considered in unrelated fashion. Plate tectonics describes seismic activity, volcanism, mountain building, and various other Earth processes in terms of the structure and mechanical behavior of a small number of enormous rigid plates thought to constitute the outer part of the planet (i.e., the lithosphere). This all-encompassing theory grew out of observations and ideas about continental drift and seafloor spreading.

In 1912, the German meteorologist Alfred Wegener proposed that throughout most of geologic time there was only one continental mass, which he named Pangea. At some time during the Mesozoic Era, Pangea divided and the parts began to drift apart. As the Americas moved west, the Atlantic Ocean opened up. The Indian block drifted across the equator to join with Asia.

In 1937, the South African Alexander Du Toit modified Wegener's hypothesis by suggesting the existence of two primordial continents: Laurasia in the north and Gondwanaland in the south. Aside from the congruence of the continental margins (the boundaries where continents meet the oceans) on both sides of the Atlantic, impressive geologic evidence supports the theory of continental drift. Similarities in fossil terrestrial organisms in pre-Cretaceous (older than about 145 million years) strata of Africa and South America and in pre-Jurassic rocks (older than about 201 million years) of Australia, India, Madagascar, and Africa are explained if these continents were formerly connected; they are otherwise

225 Million Years Ago

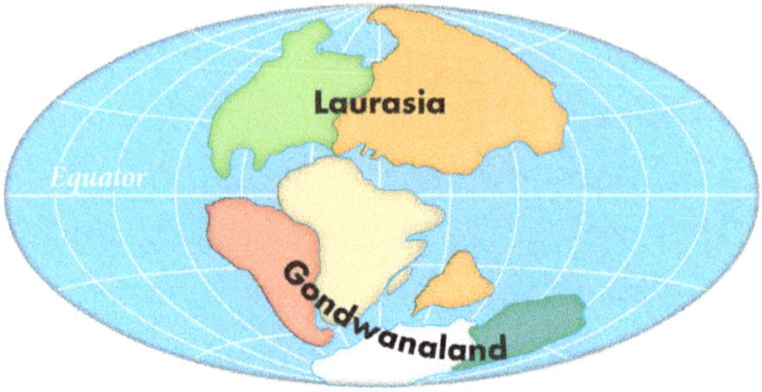

180–200 Million Years Ago

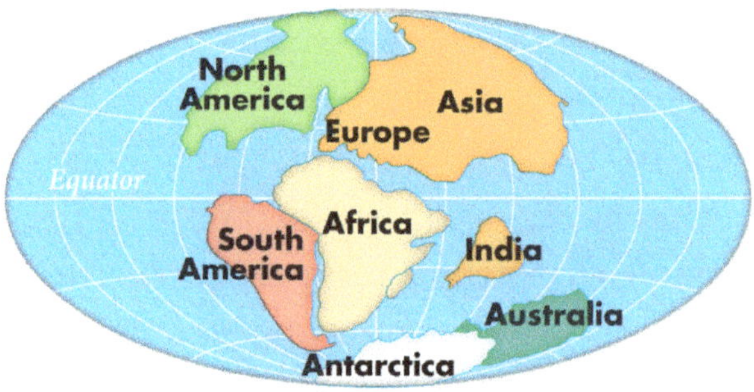

135 Million Years Ago

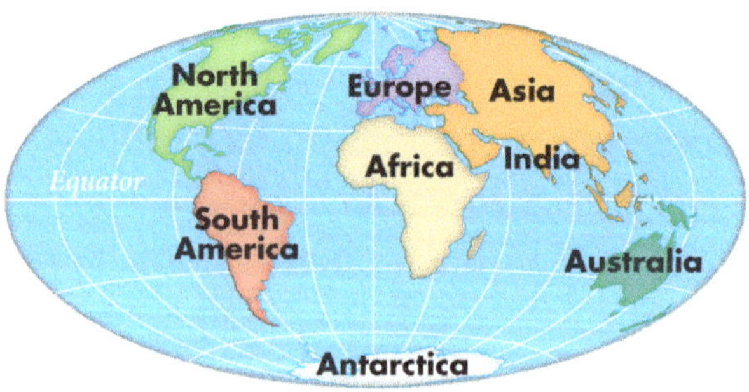

Earth Today

Four images show the location of Earth's continents at various times between 225 million years ago and the present.

difficult to explain. Fitting the Americas with the continents across the Atlantic brings together similar kinds of rocks and structures. Evidence of widespread glaciation during the late Paleozoic is found in Antarctica, southern South America, southern Africa, India, and Australia. If these continents were formerly united around the South Polar region, this glaciation can be explained as a unified sequence of events in time and space.

Interest in continental drift increased during the 1950s as knowledge of Earth's magnetic field during the geologic past developed. Ferromagnetic minerals (minerals susceptible to magnetization) acquire a permanent magnetization when they crystallize as components of igneous rock. The direction of their magnetization is the same as the direction of Earth's magnetic field at the place and time of crystallization. When weathering releases particles of magnetized minerals from their parent igneous rocks, they may later realign themselves with the existing magnetic field at the time they become incorporated into sedimentary deposits. Studies of the magnetism remaining in suitable rocks of different ages from over the world after they were no longer subject to magnetic influence indicate that the magnetic poles were in different places at different times. The polar wandering curves are different for the several continents. However, these differences are reconciled on the assumption that continents now separated were formerly joined. The curves for Europe and North America are reconciled by the assumption that America has drifted about 30° west from Europe since the Triassic period (about 252 million to 201 million years ago).

In the early 1960s, a major breakthrough in understanding the way the modern Earth works came from studies of the ocean floor. Most notably, the American geophysicists Harry H. Hess and Robert S. Dietz suggested that new ocean crust was formed along mid-oceanic ridges between separating continents.

Major advances in deep-water drilling technology provided the means to test the theory of seafloor spreading. The Joint Oceanographic Institutions Deep Earth Sampling (JOIDES) project began in 1969 and continued with various programs (since 2013, with the International Ocean Discovery Program [IODP]). These projects produced hundreds of boreholes in the floor of the world's oceans. The results have been as outstanding as plate tectonic theory, and confirm that the oceanic crust everywhere is younger than about 200 million years.

Plate tectonic theory, which embraces both continental drift and seafloor spreading, was formulated in the mid-1960s by the Canadian geologist J. Tuzo Wilson. Wilson incorporated the ideas of continental drift and seafloor spreading into his description of an evolving mosaic of enormous plates and proposed the idea of the opening and closing of oceans and eventual production of a mountainous belt by the collision of two continents.

Up to this point, no one had considered the implications of plate tectonic theory on the evolution of continental orogenic belts. Most thought had focused on the oceans. In 1969, the British geologist John Dewey examined the relationship between mountain ranges in Europe and North America in terms of a complete plate-tectonic cycle of events. In turn, this provided a model for the interpretation of other pre-Mesozoic (Paleozoic and Precambrian) belts. Even the oldest volcano-sedimentary rocks on Earth, in the 3.8 billion-year-old Isua belt in West Greenland, have been explained by geologists to have formed in a plate-tectonic setting.

HYDROLOGIC SCIENCES

Since the twentieth century, research by hydrologists into Earth's waters has been motivated by diverse interests. The growing need for fresh water for use by human as well as for resources that can be extracted from water is one motivating factor. The significant international wars of the twentieth century—notably, World War II and its Pacific arena—have given rise to the desire for a better understanding of ocean currents and depth. Finally, modern hydrology has been motivated by the need to prevent or lessen the impact of natural disasters (such as tsunamis) and climate change. As with geology, modern hydrology relies on increasingly technologically advanced equipment to achieve superior precision in its studies.

WATER RESOURCES AND SEAWATER CHEMISTRY

Studies of water distribution have revealed that astonishingly little of Earth's water is contained in lakes and rivers. Ninety-seven percent of all water is in the oceans. Of the fresh water forming the remainder, three-fourths is locked up in glacial ice and most of the rest is underground.

Approximate figures are also now available for the amounts of water involved in the different stages of the water cycle. Of the 34 inches (859 millimeters) of annual global precipitation, 23 percent falls on land. However, only one-third of the precipitation on the land runs directly back to the sea; the rest is recycled through the atmosphere by evaporation and transpiration. Groundwater below Earth's surface accumulates by infiltration of rainwater into soil and bedrock. Some may run off into rivers and lakes, and some may reemerge as springs or aquifers.

Advanced techniques are used extensively in groundwater studies nowadays. The rate of groundwater flow, for example, can be calculated from the breakdown of radioactive carbon-14 by measuring the time it takes for rainwater to pass through the ground. Numerical modeling is used to study heat and mass transfer in groundwater. High-precision equipment is used for measuring down-hole temperature, pressure, flow rate, and water level. Groundwater hydrology is important in studies of fractured reservoirs, geothermal resource exploration, radioactive waste disposal, and aquifer thermal-energy storage.

Chemical analyses of trace elements and isotopes of seawater was conducted as part of the Geochemical Ocean Sections (Geosecs) program. Of the 92 naturally occurring elements, nearly 80 were detected in seawater or in the organisms that inhabit it. The role of organisms as influences on the composition of seawater has become better understood with advances in marine biology. It is now known that plants and animals may collect certain elements to concentrations as much as 100,000 times their normal amounts in seawater. Abnormally high concentrations of beryllium, scandium, chromium, and iodine have been found in algae; of copper and arsenic in both the soft and skeletal parts of invertebrate animals; and of zirconium and cerium in plankton.

DESALINIZATION, TIDAL POWER, AND MINERALS FROM THE SEA

For ages a source of food and common salt, the sea is increasingly becoming a source of water, chemicals, and energy. In 1967, Key West, Florida, became the first US city to be supplied solely by water from the sea, drawing its supplies from a plant that produces more than 2 million gallons of refined water daily. Extraction of chemicals such as magnesia (first extracted from the Mediterranean in the late nineteenth century) is common. The first major hydrographic project for using tidal power was completed in 1967, when a dam and electrical generating equipment were installed across the Rance River in northern France.

The seafloor and the strata below the continental shelves are also sources of mineral wealth. Concretions of manganese oxide, formed as undersea volcanic rocks are weathered, have been found in dense concentrations

This desalination plant near Hadera, Israel, converts salt water from the Mediterranean Sea into drinkable water.

with a total abundance of 10^{11} tons. In addition to the manganese, these concretions contain copper, nickel, cobalt, zinc, and molybdenum. To date, oil and gas have been the most valuable products to be produced from beneath the sea.

OCEAN BATHYMETRY

Modern bathymetric charts (charts that measure water depth at various points) show that about 20 percent of the surfaces of the continents are submerged to form continental shelves. Altogether the shelves form an area about the size of Africa. Continental slopes, which slant down from the outer edges of the shelves to the plains of the seafloor, are nearly everywhere furrowed by submarine canyons. The depths to which these canyons have been cut below sea level seem to rule out the possibility that they are drowned valleys cut by ordinary streams. More likely, the canyons were eroded by turbidity currents, dense mixtures of mud and water that originate as mudslides in the heads of the canyons and pour down their bottoms.

Profiling of the Pacific basin prior to and during World War II resulted in the discovery of hundreds of isolated eminences rising more than 3,280 feet (more than 1,000 meters) above the floor. Of particular interest were seamounts in the shape of truncated cones, whose flat tops rise as much as several hundred meters below the surface. Harry H. Hess interpreted these flat-topped seamounts (guyots) as volcanic mountains planed off by action of waves before they subsided to their present depths. Subsequent drilling in guyots west of Hawaii confirmed this view; samples of rocks from the tops contained fossils of Cretaceous age representing reef-building organisms of the kind that inhabit shallow water.

Ocean Circulation, Currents, and Waves

Early in the twentieth century Vilhelm Bjerknes, a Norwegian meteorologist, and V. Walfrid Ekman, a Swedish physical oceanographer, studied the dynamics of ocean circulation and developed theories that influenced later studies of sea currents. Bjerknes showed that very small forces resulting from pressure differences caused by non-uniform seawater density could start and maintain fluid motion. Ekman analyzed the influence of winds and Earth's rotation on currents. He proposed that the frictional effects of winds blowing across the surface of water would cause movement of lower layers of water. In Ekman's theory, the deeper the currents produced by friction from winds blowing on the surface of water, the less their velocity and the greater their deflection by the Coriolis effect, until at some critical depth an induced current would move in a direction opposite to that of the wind.

Results of many studies suggest that the forces that drive the ocean currents begin at the interface between water and air. The direct transfer of momentum from the atmosphere to the sea is undoubtedly the most important driving force for currents in the upper parts of the ocean. Next in importance are differential heating, evaporation, and precipitation across the air-sea boundary, altering the density of seawater and thus initiating movement of water masses with different densities. Studies of the properties and motion of water at depth have shown that strong currents also exist in the deep sea and that distinct types of water travel far from their geographic sources. For example, the highly saline water of the Mediterranean that flows through the Strait of Gibraltar has been traced over a large part of the Atlantic, where it forms a deep-water stratum that is circulated far beyond that ocean in currents around Antarctica.

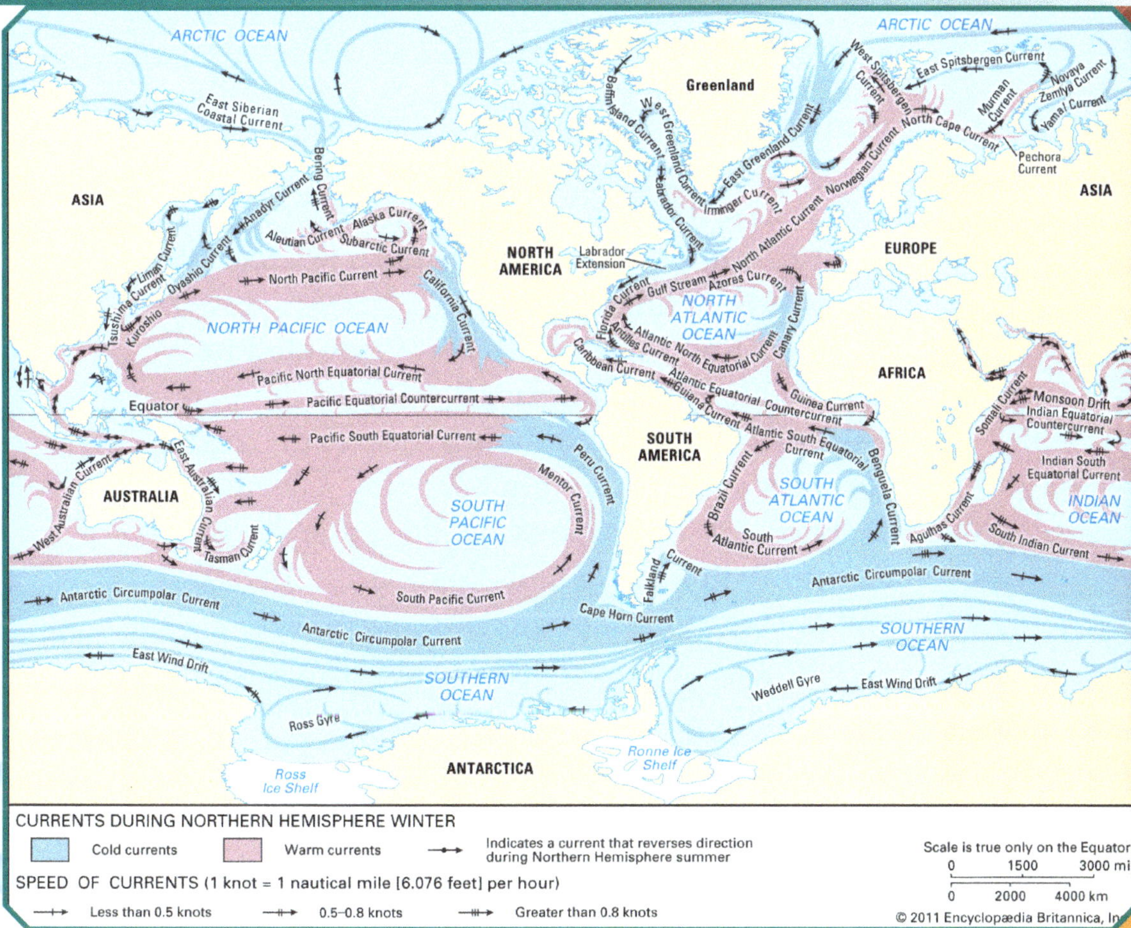

Major ocean current systems of the world

Improvements in devices for determining the motion of seawater in three dimensions have led to the discovery of new currents and to the disclosure of unexpected complexities in the circulation of the oceans generally. In 1951, a huge countercurrent moving to the east across the Pacific was found below depths as depths as shallow as 66 feet (20 meters). In the following year, a similar undercurrent was discovered near the equator in the Atlantic. In 1957, a deep countercurrent was detected beneath the Gulf Stream.

Since the 1970s, Earth-orbiting satellites have yielded much information on the temperature distribution and thermal energy of ocean currents such as the Gulf Stream. Chemical analyses from Geosecs made possible the determination of circulation paths, speeds, and mixing rates of ocean currents.

Surface waves of the ocean are also exceedingly complex, at most places and times reflecting the coexistence and interferences of several independent wave systems. During World War II, interest in forecasting wave characteristics was stimulated by the need for this critical information in the planning of amphibious operations. The oceanographers H. U. Sverdrup and Walter Heinrich Munk developed a method of forecasting "significant wave height"—the average height of the highest third of the waves in a wave train. Subsequently, this method was improved to permit wave forecasters to predict optimal routes for mariners.

Forecasting of the most destructive of all waves, tsunamis, is another recent development.

These massive waves are generated by submarine quakes and volcanic eruptions. Soon after 159 persons were killed in Hawaii by the tsunami of 1946, the US Coast and Geodetic Survey established a seismic sea-wave warning system. Using a seismic network to locate epicenters of submarine quakes, the installation predicts the arrival of tsunamis at points around the Pacific basin often hours before the arrival of the waves.

Glacier Motion and the High-Latitude Ice Sheets

Since the later 1950s, principles and techniques of metallurgy (the study of metals) and solid-state physics have been used to study the mechanics of glacial movements. Laboratory studies showed that glacial ice deforms like other crystalline solids (such as metals) at temperatures near the melting point. Continued stress produces permanent deformation. In addition to plastic deformation within a moving glacier, the glacier itself may slide over its bed by mechanisms involving pressure melting and refreezing and accelerated plastic flow around obstacles. The causes underlying changes in rate of glacial movement require further study.

As a result of numerous scientific expeditions into Greenland and Antarctica, the dimensions of the remaining great ice sheets are fairly well known. In parts of both continents it has been determined that the base of the ice is below sea level, probably due in part to the weight of the icecaps. In 1966, a borehole was drilled 4,560 feet (1,390 meters) to bedrock on the North Greenland ice sheet, and two years later a similar boring of 7,093 feet (2,162 meters) was cut through the Antarctic ice at Byrd Station. Subsequent studies revealed that the bottom layers of ice cored in Greenland were estimated to be more than 150,000 years old, compared with 100,000 years for the Antarctic core. With the advent of geochemical dating of rocks, it has become evident that the Ice Age, which in the earlier part of the century was considered to have transpired during the Quaternary period, actually began much earlier. In Antarctica, for example, potassium-argon dating of lava overlying glaciated surfaces and sedimentary deposits of glacial origin show that glaciers existed on that continent at least 10 million years ago.

The study of ice sheets has benefited from data produced by advanced instruments, computers, and orbiting satellites. The shape of ice sheets can be determined by numerical

Scientific research in polar regions, such as that which takes place at Byrd Station in Antarctica (pictured here), has revealed valuable information about icecaps and the Ice Age.

modeling, their heat budget from thermodynamic calculations, and their thickness with radar techniques. Color images from satellites show the temperature distribution across the polar regions, which can be compared with the distribution of land and sea ice.

Atmospheric Sciences

The twentieth and twenty-first centuries have witnessed immense changes to our understanding of Earth's atmosphere and how we study it. Fast-paced advances in aerospace technologies (thanks, in part, to the Cold War–era space race) have allowed scientists to collect data from outer space and to travel through Earth's atmosphere. The greatest impact of such advanced atmospheric study has been on aircraft and spacecraft and on meteorology.

PROBES, SATELLITES, AND DATA TRANSMISSION

Kites equipped with meteorographs (devices that simultaneously measure air pressure, temperature, moisture, and other atmospheric data) were used as atmospheric probes in the late 1890s. In 1907, the US Weather Bureau recorded the ascent of a kite to 23,110 feet (7,044 meters) above Mount Weather, Virginia.

In the 1920s, the radio replaced the telegraph and telephone as the primary instrument for collecting weather data. By 1936, the radio meteorograph (radiosonde) was developed, with capabilities of sending signals on relative humidity, temperature, and barometric pressure from unmanned balloons. Experimentation with balloons up to heights of about 19 miles (31 kilometers) showed that columns of warm air may rise more than 1 mile

(1.6 kilometers) above Earth's surface and that the lower atmosphere is often layered, with winds in the different layers blowing in different directions.

During the 1930s, airplanes began to be used for observations of the weather. Since 1945, the development of rockets and weather satellites has also occurred. TIROS (Television Infra-Red Observation Satellite), the world's first all-weather satellite, was launched in 1960, and in 1964, the Nimbus Satellite of the United States National Aeronautics and Space Administration (NASA) was rocketed into near-polar orbit.

There are two types of weather satellites: polar and geostationary. Polar satellites, like Nimbus, orbit Earth at low altitudes of a few hundred kilometers. Because of their progressive drift, polar satellites produce a photographic coverage of the entire Earth every twenty-four hours. Geostationary satellites, first launched in 1966, are above the equator at heights of about 21,748 miles (35,000 kilometers). They transmit data at regular intervals. Much information can be derived from the data collected by satellites. For example, wind speed and direction are measured from cloud paths, while atmospheric temperature and moisture are calculated from infrared data.

GOES-8, a US weather satellite, 1994

WEATHER FORECASTING

Efforts at incorporating numerical data on weather into mathematical formulas that could then be used for forecasting began early in the twentieth century at the Norwegian Geophysical Institute. Vilhelm Bjerknes successfully devised equations to relate the components of weather that could be measured. However, the complexity of the equations meant they did not provide the rapid solutions needed for forecasting. Out

JOHN VON NEUMANN

John von Neumann (1903–1957) was a US mathematician who made an important contribution to the development of the hydrogen bomb through his work on high-speed calculators. Born in Budapest, Hungary, on Dec. 28, 1903, von Neumann moved to the United States in 1930 and became a citizen in 1937. He worked as a research professor of mathematics at the Institute for Advanced Study, Princeton, New Jersey, and served on the Atomic Energy Commission from 1954 to 1957.

In addition to his work on high-speed calculating machines, von Neumann was an expert on games of strategy and their application to economic behavior; he also did much pioneering work in the areas of logical design of computers, methods of programming, the problem of designing reliable machines using unreliable components, machine imitation of randomness, and the problem of constructing machines that can reproduce their own kind. He died on Feb. 8, 1957, in Washington, DC.

of his team's efforts, however, came the polar front theory for the origin of cyclones and the now-familiar names of cold front, warm front, and stationary front for the leading edges of air masses.

In 1922, the British mathematician Lewis Fry Richardson demonstrated that Bjerknes's complex equations could be reduced to long series of simple arithmetic operations.

The simplicity of mathematical tools at the time, however, made the solution of a problem an issue of manpower. In 1946, the Hungarian-American mathematician John von Neumann started work on an electronic device to do computations faster than weather developed. Four years later, the von Neumann group could claim that, given adequate data, their computer could forecast the weather as well as a human weather forecaster. Present-day weather forecasting is achieved with the help of advanced computer analysis.

CLOUD PHYSICS

Studies of cloud physics have shown that the centers around which water condenses vary widely in terms of concentration and areal distribution, ranging from six per cubic centimeter over the oceans to more than 4 million per cubic centimeter in the polluted air of some cities. The droplets that condense on these foreign particles may be as small as 0.0004 inch (0.001 centimeter) in diameter. Raindrops apparently may form directly from the converging of these droplets, as in the case of tropical rains, or in the temperate zones through the intermediary of ice crystals. According to the theory of German meteorologists Tor Bergson and Walter Findeisen, vapor freezing on ice crystals in the clouds enlarges the crystals until they fall. What finally hits the ground depends on the temperature of air below the cloud—if below freezing, snow; if above, rain.

PROPERTIES AND STRUCTURE OF THE ATMOSPHERE

Early in the space age in 1958, the US satellite Explorer I was sent into orbit with a device to measure the intensity of cosmic radiation at different levels above the ground. At heights around 621 miles (1,000 kilometers) the instrument stopped working as a result of saturation by charged particles. This and subsequent research showed that a zone of radiation encircles the world between about latitude 75°N and 75°S, with maximum intensities at 3,106 and 9,942 miles (5,000 and 16,000 kilometers). Named the Van Allen region, these zones are responsive to events taking place on the sun. The solar wind, a stream of atomic particles emanating from the sun in all directions, seems to be responsible for the electrons entrapped in the Van Allen region as well as for the teardrop shape of the magnetosphere (the magnetic field surrounding Earth) as a whole, with its tail pointing always away from the sun.

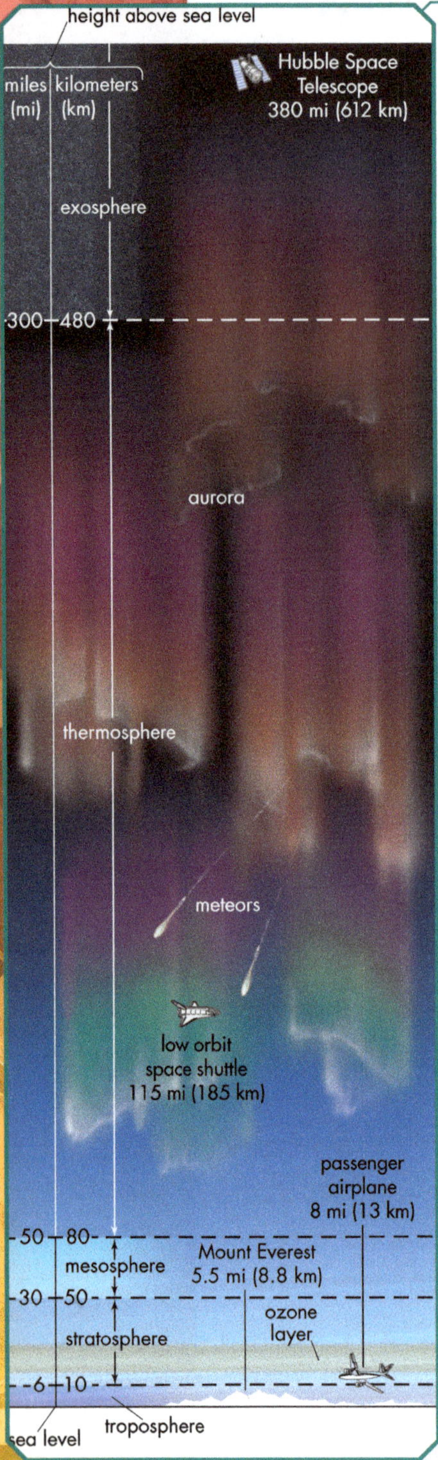

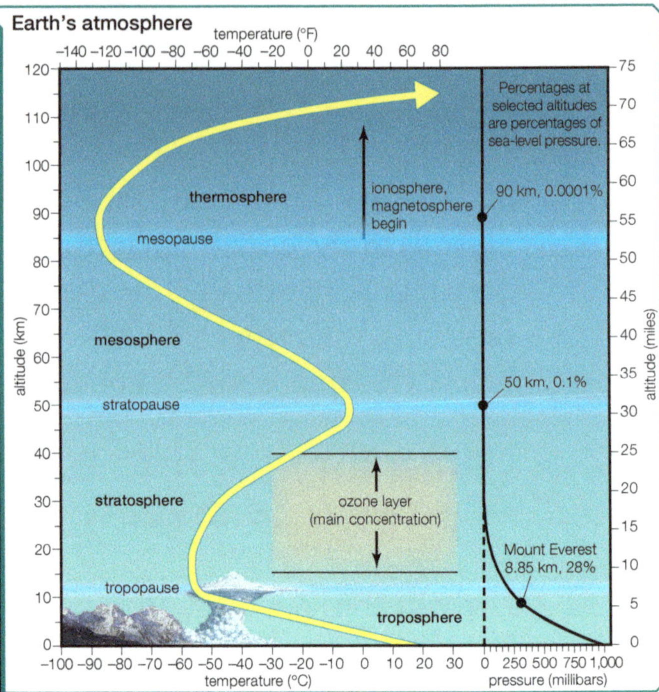

In 1898, the French meteorologist Teisserenc de Bort discovered that, at elevations of about 7 miles (11 kilometers), the figure for average decrease of temperature with height (about 5.5°C per 1,000 meters of ascent) dropped and the value remained nearly constant at around -67°F (-55°C). He named the atmospheric zones below and above this temperature boundary the troposphere and the stratosphere.

Earth's atmosphere is divided into distinct layers defined by changes in air temperature with increasing height. Most of Earth's clouds, and most weather events, occur in the lowest layer, the trophosphere.

Toward the end of World War II, the B-29 Superfortress came into use as the first large aircraft to cruise regularly at 32,808 feet (10,000 meters). Flying toward the west from bases in the Pacific, these planes sometimes encountered unexpected head winds that slowed their flight by as much as 186 miles (300 kilometers) per hour. The jet streams, as these high-altitude winds were named, have been found to encircle Earth following wavy courses and moving from west to east at velocities ranging upward to 311 miles (500 kilometers) per hour.

Aircraft have also proved useful in studies of the structure and dynamics of tropical hurricanes. Following the destruction on the Atlantic Coast of the United States in 1955 by hurricanes Connie and Diane, a national center was established in Florida with the missions of locating and tracking and, it is hoped, of learning how to predict the paths of hurricanes and to dissipate their energy.

WEATHER MODIFICATION

As late as the 1890s, experiments were conducted in the United States in the hope of producing rain by setting off charges of dynamite lofted by balloons or kites. No positive results were reported, however. More promising were the cloud-seeding experiments of the 1940s, in which silver iodide was released into clouds as smoke or solid carbon dioxide was broadcast into clouds from airplanes. The results are still uncertain for increasing precipitation. The lessons learned from cloud seeding, however, have had other successful applications, such as the dispersal of low-level fog at airports (the first system designed for this purpose was set up in 1970 at Orly airport in Paris).

The inadvertent weather modification caused by industrialization and the building of large cities has already produced measurable changes in local climate and may someday produce effects more widespread. The introduction of billions of tons of carbon dioxide into the atmosphere each year from the burning of fuels has been connected with an increase in Earth's average temperature. Cities affect the flow of wind, warm the atmosphere over them, and send pollutants into the sky. Updrafts may increase rainfall and winter fog and reduce sunshine and daylight.

CONCLUSION

As earth scientists in all fields continue to pursue more advanced, specialized studies of all natural phenomena on Earth, it is worthy to note the interconnectedness of such systems. Earth's features—its atmosphere, oceans, ice masses, land surfaces, and vegetation—are linked and mutually influence each other in complex ways that we often do not fully comprehend. Together, these features make up an integrated Earth system, in which all components interact with and influence one another. As specialization yields more complex, rich data about specific features of Earth, we must remain mindful of the overall picture. It is the task of earth scientists to reach a full understanding of the complex feedback and interactions among the various components of Earth's systems.

In the twenty-first century, the earth scientist's task has become increasingly central to the survival of Earth's species. The rise of air temperatures near Earth's surface over the past century is attributed by virtually all reputable scientists to human causes. As earth scientists further develop their understanding of how Earth's interrelated systems operate on each other, they can pinpoint with better specificity the broad impact of specific human actions. In turn, governments and research organizations can enact progressive, responsible policies to eliminate such threats to Earth's natural systems. This is the most pressing task faced by earth scientists in the twenty-first century.

alchemy A medieval chemical science with the goals of changing less valuable metals into gold, discovering a single cure for all diseases, and discovering how to live forever.

alloy A substance consisting of two or more metals or of a metal and a nonmetal united, usually by being melted together.

ammonite Any of numerous flat spiral fossil shells of mollusks related to the nautilus that were especially abundant in the Mesozoic era of geological history.

aquifer A water-bearing layer of rock, sand, or gravel capable of absorbing water.

Babylonia Ancient country in valley of lower Euphrates and Tigris Rivers; capital, Babylon.

bore A tidal flood with a high abrupt front.

centrifuge A machine using centrifugal force for separating substances of different densities, for removing moisture, or for simulating gravitational effects.

condense To change from a less dense to a denser form.

congruence The quality or state of having the same size and shape.

convection Motion in a gas or liquid in which the warmer portions rise and the colder portions sink.

Coriolis force An apparent force that, as a result of Earth's rotation, deflects moving objects or air currents to the right in the Northern Hemisphere and to the left in the Southern Hemisphere.

erratic A boulder or block of rock transported from its original resting place, especially by a glacier.

faunal Of or relating to animals or animal life, especially of a region, period, or environment.

Genesis The first book of the Jewish and Christian scriptures.

hydrology A science dealing with the characteristics, distribution, and circulation of water on and below the surface of the land and in the atmosphere.

inert Unable or slow to move, act, or react.

mineralogy The scientific study of the characteristics and classification of minerals.

multidisciplinary Of or relating to an approach that branches multiple fields of study.

naturalist A person who specializes in natural history.

orogeny The process of mountain formation, especially by folding of Earth's crust.

paleontology A science dealing with the life of past geological periods as known especially from fossil remains.

perforate To make a hole or series of holes through.

petrology A science that deals with the origin, history, occurrence, structure, chemical composition, and classification of rocks.

phenomenon A fact, feature, or event of scientific interest.

prospect To explore, especially for mineral deposits.

seismograph A device to measure and record vibrations of the earth.

stratum A layer of a substance; one of a series of layers.

till A mixture of clay, sand, gravel, and boulders deposited by a glacier.

topographic Of or relating to the shape and height and depth of the features of a place.

treatise A book or article examining a subject carefully and completely.

American Geosciences Institute (AGI)
4220 King Street
Alexandria, VA 22302
(703) 379-2480
Website: http://www.agiweb.org
Founded in 1948 as an initiative of the National Academy of Sciences, the AGI is a network of associations that provides information for geoscientists and fosters earth science education.

American Institute of Hydrology (AIH)
Engineering D—Mail Code 6603
Southern Illinois University Carbondale
1230 Lincoln Drive
Carbondale, IL 62901
(618) 453-7809
Website: http://www.aihydrology.org
The AIH is the only nationwide organization that offers certification to qualified professionals in all fields of the hydrological sciences.

American Museum of Natural History (AMNH)
Central Park West at 79th Street

New York, NY 10024
(212) 769-5100
Website: http://www.amnh.org
The AMNH is one of the most preeminent scientific and cultural institutions in the world. Its exhibits on human culture and the natural world are unparalleled.

American Water Resources Association (AWRA)
PO Box 1626
Middleburg, VA 20118
(540) 687-8390
Website: http://www.awra.org
The AWRA's goal is to educate the public about water resources and related issues.

Canadian Meteorological and Oceanographic Society (CMOS)
PO Box 3211
Station D
Ottawa, ON K1P 6H7
Canada
(613) 990-0300
Website: http://www.cmos.ca
The CMOS is dedicated to advancing

atmospheric and oceanic sciences and related environmental disciplines in Canada.

Geological Association of Canada (GAC)
c/o Department of Earth Sciences
Room ER4063
Alexander Murray Building
Memorial University of Newfoundland
St. John's, NL A1B 3X5
Canada
(709) 864-7660
Website: https://www.gac.ca
The GAC is dedicated to promoting the study of geoscience in Canada through publications, meetings, and the numerous medals and awards it bestows upon researchers and students.

Geological Society of America (GSA)
PO Box 9140
Boulder, CO 80301
(303) 357-1000
Website: http://www.geosociety.org
Since 1888, the GSA has aimed to provide resources for earth science studies in all sectors—private, governmental, and academic. Its membership includes over 26,000 individuals in over 115 countries.

National Center for Atmospheric Research (NCAR)
PO Box 3000
Boulder, CO 80307
(303) 497-1000
Website: https://ncar.ucar.edu
NCAR is a federally funded research facility dedicated to the atmospheric sciences.

Websites

Because of the changing nature of internet links, Rosen Publishing has developed an online list of websites related to the subject of this book. This site is updated regularly. Please use this link to access the list:

http://www.rosenlinks.com/SCI/Earth

FOR FURTHER READING

Anderson, Michael, ed. *Investigating Earth's Oceans*. New York, NY: Britannica Educational Publishing, 2012.

Anderson, Michael, ed. *Investigating Earth's Weather*. New York, NY: Britannica Educational Publishing, 2012.

Anderson, Michael, ed. *Investigating the Global Climate*. New York, NY: Britannica Educational Publishing, 2012.

Anderson, Michael, ed. *Investigating the History of Earth*. New York, NY: Britannica Educational Publishing, 2012.

Anderson, Michael, ed. *Investigating Minerals, Rocks, and Fossils*. New York, NY: Britannica Educational Publishing, 2012.

Anderson, Michael, ed. *Investigating Plate Tectonics, Earthquakes, and Volcanoes*. New York, NY: Britannica Educational Publishing, 2012.

Challoner, Jack. *Rocks & Minerals: Crystals, Erosion, Geology, Fossils*. London, UK: Armadillo, 2015.

Farndon, John. *Planet Earth: Continents, Oceans, Climate, Geology*. London, UK: Armadillo, 2014.

Faulkner, Nicholas, ed. *Oceanography and Hydrology*. New York, NY: Britannica Educational Publishing, 2016.

Gray, Leon. *The Science of Tsunamis*. New York, NY: Gareth Stevens Publishing, 2013.

Gregory, Josh. *Hydrologist* (Cool STEM Careers). Ann Arbor, MI: Cherry Lake Publishing, 2013.

Harris, Tim. *Earth Science* (Science Q&A). New York, NY: Cavendish Square, 2016.

Mullins, Matt. *Geoscientist* (Cool STEM Careers). Ann Arbor, MI: Cherry Lake Publishing, 2013.

INDEX

A

Abbot, Henry Larcom, 70
Agassiz, Louis, 58–61
Agricola, Georgius, 31, 32–33
air/atmosphere circulation, 46–47
alchemy, 31
Anaxagoras of Clazomenae, 25
Anaximander of Miletus, 22
Aristotle, 14, 15, 20, 22, 23–24
atmospheric composition and structure, 76–77, 125–127
atmospheric sciences
  in the 19th century, 75–86
  in the 16th to 18th centuries, 42–47
  in the 20th century to present, 119–128

B

barometer, invention of, 46
bathymetry, 112–113
Beagle, 68, 71
Berzelius, Jöns Jacob, 50
Bjerknes, Vilhelm, 113, 122, 123
Boltwood, Bertram, 88, 89
Bouguer, Pierre, 66
Bowen, Norman L., 92–93
Bragg, William Henry, 94–96
Bridgman, P. W., 93
Buchan, Alexander, 83–84, 85

C

catastrophism, doctrine of, 55–56
Caxton, Willliam, 16
Challenger, 68, 73
Clausius, Rudolf, 76
clouds/cloud physics, 45–46, 77–78, 124–125
Coulier, Paul-Jean, 78
creation story, 12
crystallography, 49, 94–96
Cuvier, Baron Georges, 55–56

D

Dalton, John, 76
Dampier, William, 79
Dana, James Dwight, 50
Darcy, Henri-Philibert-G aspard, 68, 69
Darcy's law, 69
Darwin, Charles, 57, 62, 63, 71
Davis, William Morris, 64–66
De Lapidibus, 13
Democritus of Abdera, 27
Descartes, René, 39, 43, 46
Dewey, John, 107
Dietz, Robert S., 106
Diogenes of Apollonia, 25
discharge of streams, 70
Discours admirables, 40
Dittmar, Wilhelm, 74
Dove, Heinrich Wilhelm, 79

Dupuit, Arsène-Jules-Étienne-Juvénal, 69
Dutton, Clarence Edward, 67

E

Earth, age of, 61–63
Earth history, two major theories of, 38–39
Ekman, V. Walfrid, 113, 114
Empedocles of Agrigentum, 22
Epistles of the Brethren of Purity and Loyal Friends, 20
Eratosthenes, 26–27
erratics, 58, 59
Espy, James Pollard, 81
Essay Towards a Natural History of the Earth and Terrestrial Bodies, 40
Études sur les glaciers, 59
evaporation of sea water, 41–42
Evolution of the Igneous Rocks, 93
experimental study of rocks/petrology, 92–94

F

faunal succession, law of, 49, 51–56, 61
Ferrel, William, 75
Forchheimer, Philip, 69–70
Franklin, Benjamin, 46

G

geochronology, 13, 89–90
Geological Survey, 70
Geologic Map of England and Wales with Part of Scotland, 52
geologic time, 61–63
geology/geologic sciences
  in the 19th century, 48–67
  origins/history of, 13–21
  in the 16th to 18th centuries, 30–39
  in the 20th century to present, 88–107
  what it is, 12–13
geomorphic cycle, 64–66
Gilbert, Grove Karl, 64
glacial motion, 117–119
glacial theory/ice age, 58–61
groundwater, 28–29, 67, 68, 69–70, 109–110
Guericke, Otto von, 43, 44–45, 77

H

Hall, James, 67
Halley, Edmond, 41–42
Häuy, René-Just, 49
Hecataeus of Miletus, 25
Henry, Joseph, 82
Herbertson, Andrew John, 86
Herodotus, 18
Hess, Harry H., 106, 113
Hooke, Robert, 37

Howard, Luke, 77
Hubbert, Marion King, 94
Humboldt, Alexander von, 85
Humphreys, Andrew Atkinson, 70
Hutton, James, 38–39
hydrology/hydrologic sciences
  in the 19th century, 67–75
  origins/history of, 21–29
  in the 16th to 18th centuries, 39–42
  in the 20th century to present, 108–119

I

ice age/glacial theory, 58–61
isostasy, 67

J

Jefferson, Thomas, 71
Jinshu, 18–20
Joint Oceanographic Institutions Deep Earth Sampling (JOIDES), 106

K

Kelvin, Lord/William Thomson, 63, 89
Kircher, Athanasius, 40

L

Lambert, Johann Heinrich, 46
landform evolution, 64–66
Lister, Martin, 51
Loomis, Elias, 79, 82, 86
Lüshi chunqiu, 22
Lyceum, 14
Lyell, Charles, 56–58, 63

M

Mariotte, Edmé, 41
mass spectrometer, 89
Maury, Matthew Fontaine, 71
meteorology, 82–86
micropaleontology, 97–98
Milne, John, 99
mineralogy, 31–33, 49–51
Mirrour of the World, 16
Mississippi Delta Survey, 70
Mohorovičić, Andrija, 99, 100
Murray, John, 73

N

National Ocean Survey, 71
Neptunian theory of Earth history, 38–39
Neumann, John von, 123, 124
New Voyage Round the World, 79
Nicol, William, 51
Nile River, origin of, 24–27

O

ocean circulation, 113–116
oceanography, foundations of, 71–75
Oenopides of Chios, 25

P

paleontology, 13, 33–38
Palissy, Bernard, 40
Perrault, Pierre, 41
Physical Geography of the Sea, 71
Piddington, Henry, 81
plate tectonics, 102–107
Plato, 22–23
Playfair, John, 39
Plot, Robert, 40
Plutonian theory of Earth history, 38–39
Poseidonius, 27
Powell, John Wesley, 64
Principles of Geology, 56, 57, 58

R

radiometric dating, 88–92
Ramberg, Hans, 94
Redfield, William C., 80
Reid, William, 81
Report on the Geology of the Henry Mountains, 64
Richardson, Lewis Fry, 123
Royal Society, 37, 51, 53
Rubey, Willliam W., 94

S

Saussure, Horace Bénédict de, 47, 58
seismology, 99–102
Shen Kuo, 18
Smith, William, 52–55
Sorby, Clifton, 51
steady-state theory, 56–58
Steno, Nicolaus, 33–37
storms, observation and study of, 79–82
Strabo, 15
Strata Identified by Organized Fossils, 52
stratigraphy, 33–38
stream gauging, 70
subterranean water, rise of, 39–41
superposition, law of, 37, 61
System of Mineralogy, 50

T

Teisserenc de Bort, Léon-Philippe, 85, 126
Thales of Miletus, 21–22, 24
Theophrastus, 13, 14–15
Thomson, William/Lord Kelvin, 63, 89
tides, early knowledge of, 27–28
tsunamis, forecasting, 116–117

U

uniformitarianism, theory of, 56–58, 63
US Coast Survey, 71

V

van 't Hoff, Jacobus Henricus, 92
Vitruvius, 28–29

W

water cycle, development of idea, 22–24
water vapor in atmosphere, understanding of, 43–45
weather
  forecasting, 76, 122–124
  maps, 82–86
  modification, 127–128
  satellites, 121
Wegener, Alfred, 103
Werner, Abraham Gottlob, 33, 38
Wilson, J. Tuzo, 107
Woodward, John, 40

X

Xenophanes of Colophon, 17

Z

Zhang Heng, 16, 17
Zheng Sixiao, 15
Zirkel, Ferdinand, 51